Backpacking & The Path of Life

By
Dwayne Weaver

Copyright © 2024 by Dwayne Weaver. All rights reserved.
Tremendous Leadership PO Box 267 • Boiling Springs, PA 17007
(717) 701 - 8159 • (800) 233 - 2665
www.TremendousLeadership.com

Scripture quotations marked (NLT) are taken from the *Holy Bible*, New Living Translation, copyright ©1996, 2004, 2015 by Tyndale House Foundation. Used by permission of Tyndale House Publishers, Carol Stream, Illinois 60188. All rights reserved.

Scripture quotations marked (NIV) are taken from the Holy Bible, New International Version®, NIV®. Copyright © 1973, 1978, 1984, 2011 by Biblica, Inc.™ Used by permission of Zondervan. All rights reserved worldwide www.zondervan.com. The "NIV" and "New International Version" are trademarks registered in the United States Patent and Trademark Office by Biblica, Inc.™

Tremendous Leadership's titles may be purchased in bulk for business or promotional use or for special sales. Please contact Tremendous Leadership for more information. Tremendous Leadership and its logo are trademarks of Tremendous Leadership. All rights reserved. No part of this publication may be reproduced, stored in or introduced into a retrieval system, or transmitted in any form, or by any means (electronic, mechanical, photocopying, recording, or otherwise) without prior written permission of both the copyright owner and the above publisher of this book except by a reviewer who wishes to quote brief passages.

The advice and recommendations presented in this book are based on the personal experiences and opinions of the author, Dwayne Weaver. While every effort has been made to ensure the accuracy and usefulness of the information provided, it is intended for general guidance only. Readers are strongly encouraged to conduct their own research, seek professional advice, and take appropriate safety measures before engaging in any hiking, backpacking, or outdoor activity.

Hiking and backpacking are inherently risky activities that may involve exposure to unpredictable weather, wildlife, and challenging terrain. The author and publisher disclaim any liability for injuries, accidents, or damages that may result from the use or misuse of the information contained in this book. Readers are responsible for their own safety and should take all necessary precautions, including proper training, physical preparation, and equipment checks, before embarking on any outdoor adventure.

Jetboil® is registered trademark of Johnson Outdoors, Inc. (Johnson Outdoors). Neither the Author, this Book, or its contents are associated, endorsed, or sponsored by Johnson Outdoors.

Paperback ISBN 978-1-961202-35-1
eBook ISBN 978-1-961202-36-8

Appendix 3 Backpack Illustration by Cynthia Weaver.

DESIGNED & PRINTED IN THE UNITED STATES OF AMERICA

TABLE OF CONTENTS

From The Author v
Introduction ix

Chapter 1 – First Time Backpacking 1
Chapter 2 – Trekking Poles 11
Chapter 3 – On Our Own 17
Chapter 4 – All for One 25
Chapter 5 – A Change of Plans 33
Chapter 6 – Backpacking with Cindy 41
Chapter 7 – Hundred Mile Wilderness 51
Chapter 8 – Trail Food 61
Chapter 9 – Sharing the Passion 69
Chapter 10 – The Full Backpack 77
Chapter 11 – Hiking with Your Eyes Open 87
Chapter 12 – The Reward 95
Chapter 13 – Glacier 103
Chapter 14 – The Bucket List 113
Chapter 15 – Old Loggers Path 121
Chapter 16 – Spring Surprise 129
Chapter 17 – Lighten Your Load 139
Chapter 18 – Why I Backpack 149
Epilogue 163

Appendix One – Backpacking Handout for Newbie 167
Appendix Two – Backpack Packing List 171
Appendix Three – Backpack Illustration 175
About the Author................................ 177

FROM THE AUTHOR

I didn't start backpacking until I was 45, but it quickly became my passion. I have enjoyed the outdoors since childhood, when I spent my summers exploring and playing in the woods. As a teen, I was part of a 4-H group that did long-distance trail rides on horseback. As an adult, I picked up the hobby of fly fishing, which I still enjoy doing today. As I reflect on my past outdoor experiences, backpacking connected all the dots for me and kept me wanting more.

This collection of short stories is not a "how-to" book, leaving the reader with all the knowledge they will need to begin or advance in backpacking. However, whether the reader is a novice or seasoned backpacker, I hope they pick up some tidbits to help them on the trail. This book is also not meant to be a "where-to" book, giving readers a list of my recommendations for the ten best trails to backpack. Nonetheless, I present various trails that may whet your appetite for what trail you want to backpack next. If you decide to hike one of the trails I mentioned in a story, I recommend you research before hitting the trail. Trail routes change, guidelines such as the need for permits change, and you must get up-to-date information as you plan your trip.

Instead, I want to give you an escape from the routine of a busy life—when you are too busy to go backpacking and want a little taste of what you enjoy doing when you have the time. Also, I hope you can connect with my stories because you have previously hiked the same trail or because you have had a similar experience backpacking. Nothing will thrill me more than if you say to yourself, "I know what he is saying; I have experienced the same thing!"

One common thread in all of these stories is the role of planning when it comes to backpacking. Planning is an essential aspect of backpacking because it helps you anticipate what you will need while on the trail and enables you to experience a safer hike. I am a natural planner, which is one reason I connect with backpacking so well.

In most of these stories, I mention a piece of backpacking equipment that I owned or had to purchase. I am a backpacking equipment fanatic, and it is hard to resist buying the newest and probably the lightest version of equipment on the market.

You will also see that I draw a parallel between backpacking and my spiritual journey in each of the stories. For me, there is a spiritual component to backpacking and hiking. Being in the woods is where I feel the closest to God and spiritually refreshed. It is an opportunity to disconnect from the world's wires and connect with God and his creation. When I am backpacking, my daily routine is to pack up camp in the morning, mount the backpack on my back, hold my trekking

From the Author

poles, gather the group in a circle, sometimes share scripture, and always pray before we start hiking for the day.

My professional career journey has taken a few unusual turns. I graduated from college with a degree in business and accounting and spent the next 20 years behind a desk, honing my skills as an accountant and financial manager. My wife, Cindy, and I have always been active in our local church by helping with the youth and children. I was the Program Director of a camp for underprivileged children for three summers, and Cindy was the Chapel Coordinator. The camp was a "fresh-air" venue for inner-city children to experience God's creation in a camp setting. During the summers, we raised our family in a four-room cottage at the campground.

I began pursuing an online degree for ministry and once attained, I resigned as the Vice-President of Finance for the company I was employed by and served as a full-time Children's Pastor for the next seven years. While I cherish the years I invested in children's ministry, it became apparent that this season of my life had ended. I accepted a position as the Chief Financial Officer and later as the Chief Executive Officer of the same construction company. My backpacking journey began when I was a Children's Pastor and continued as the construction company employed me.

I thank my wife, Cindy, for being the initial editor of this book and for her patience while reading and re-reading what I had written. More than that, I thank Cindy for her willingness to share in my passion for backpacking and for being my favorite backpacking buddy!

I also want to thank Reverend Lee Rogers and Reverend George Krebs, who reviewed my stories and scriptural applications. Pastor Lee is a friend, fellow backpacker, and author. Pastor George is a friend, mentor, and flyfishing companion.

Their critiques and comments were very valuable and precious to me.

Lastly, I want to mention what a joy it was to work with the publishing team at Tremendous Leadership. Tracey Jones was so tremendously patient and inciteful as she guided me through the writing and publishing process!

My resource for these stories is a plastic storage bin where I keep my maps, trail guides, and trail notes. Thankfully, I was diligent about taking photos of each hike, and they were an invaluable record of the sights and people that have been part of my backpacking journey. Please feel free to contact me through the contact page of www.backpackingandthepathoflife.com. There are some downloadable resources available on the website as well. I hope you enjoy reading these stories as much as I enjoyed remembering my time backpacking and my journey on the path of life.

INTRODUCTION

Consider the backpacking trail. Without the trail, backpacking as we know it would not exist. You could have a starting point and hack through the wilderness to a finishing point, but that would be bushwhacking, not backpacking. The trail, while not without its challenges, leads you on a journey through miles of wilderness beauty.

You spent the night beside a transparent meadow stream. Its soothing voice was the last thing you heard as you drifted off to sleep. As the day awakened, you put one foot in front of the other on rough-hewn logs that helped you traverse a fern-filled bog. The bog transitioned to a leaf-covered soil trail, and now that you no longer had to concentrate on where you were placing your feet, you looked up and saw an imposing mountain that you realized had to be soon scaled. For now, you were casually walking under the shade of some hardwood trees and following an old railroad bed. Suddenly—the trail took a quick turn, and you were clearly on the first leg of a switchback up the mountain grade. The switchback began as a dirt and clay surface trail with an occasional rock that you had to navigate around but grew to be primarily rocks and then all rocks. The tap, scratch, and click of your trekking poles were spaced further apart as your pace slowed and slowed. It was time for a break. You didn't realize how hard your heart was working until you stood still and could hear and feel each pump. You took a few sips and then gulps of water as your heart slowly returned to its regular beat. You looked up and realized you were only one-quarter of the way to the summit. You calculated that you would take at least two more breaks before reaching the top. Break number two. Break number three. Summit. Break number four.

There is now mostly rock and some clay soil. Soon, it is all soil with a dusting of pine needles. The aroma is distinct and draws to the surface of your mind prior climbs and prior hikes and just an overall sense of calm and peacefulness. There are rock cairns that lead you to the rock outcropping, where you will break for lunch. You follow each pile of rocks in anticipation of what the view might be like. You arrive at the mountain vista, and it is beyond words, which it usually is. It is here where all of God's creation is on full display. It is a morning's journey made possible by the trail.

There are an estimated 87,834 miles of trails in the National Trail System and 158,000 miles of trails within the US Forest Service. This number does not include the additional state, regional, and local trails available for recreational hiking.[1] The hiking and backpacking opportunities are unlimited.

---

[1] "Hiking Trails in America." America Hiking Society, www.americanhiking.org/wp-content/uploads/2015/05/AHS_RPT_fnl_LOW.pdf (November 9, 2023)

Introduction

Consider the trail maintainer. While some are federal or state employees, most are volunteers who faithfully and with great passion create, relocate, and maintain the trails that we are privileged to enjoy. Have you ever tried to grow a garden and been frustrated by the persistence of the weeds growing where they are not supposed to grow? It is not natural for man to determine where the trail is to go and then for nature to cooperate with the decision. Considering the effort it takes to maintain the thousands of miles of trails, it is incredible that I have only encountered trail maintainers on two occasions.

My first encounter with a trail maintainer was hiking the "Hundred Mile Wilderness" in Maine. It was the third day of a five-day hike, and we would spend the night at the Cloud Pond shelter. We passed the trail maintainer while he painted a white blaze on a rock to mark the trail. He was a physically fit middle-aged man using his vacation time to maintain "his" section of the trail. We could later see his rough camp, set up several hundred yards from the shelter where we were comfortably situated for the night.

My second encounter with a trail maintainer was hiking the Quehanna Trail in Elk County, Pennsylvania. We were on a steep descent and came upon a tree that had fallen over the trail. Once we reached the other side of the tree, we discovered an older woman carrying a chainsaw who was getting ready to remove the obstruction. She was in her late 50s or early 60s, and the amazing thing is that she had a physical handicap that only gave her full use of one of her legs. It took her great effort to maneuver on the trail. When we spoke to her, she referred to the trail with great affection. This trail was her life; she loved it, and it was her joy to maintain it.

Only two encounters, yet I have seen—hundreds of felled trees cut through to allow for access on the trail, miles of logs laid end to end to elevate the trail above marshy bogs, technically designed erosion barriers to reduce runoff damage, and switchbacks contoured out of the side of the mountain to make it easier to hike steep grades. My lack of encounters does not reveal a shortage of trail maintainers, but it is evidence of the many trail miles available to hike. There are so many miles of trail that the probability of a hiker and maintainer crossing paths is very low. As a backpacker, I greatly appreciate the sacrifice of these trail maintainers who serve us through their selfless commitment.

Trails make the arduous journey easier; sometimes, getting from the starting point to the finish line is only possible with the trail. Notice, I didn't say that the trail makes the journey **easy**; I said the trail makes the journey **easier**. No matter how splendid the trail is, backpacking is difficult. You carry 30-plus pounds on your back while ascending and descending a mountain grade. Your body is suffering from sore knees, foot blisters, and overworked muscles not used to this activity. Inevitably, it will rain, and you will get wet, either from the rain or by your sweat, as your rain gear traps in your body heat. The summer adds bugs, heat, humidity, and a lack of drinking water. The things I just mentioned are expected, but there is also the unexpected. Challenges such as making a wrong turn and losing your way, getting sick while on the trail, turning an ankle when collecting firewood, or discovering that a spring you were counting on was now dry may all have to be navigated while on the trail.

Consider life. It starts as a newborn baby with its eyes latched onto its parent's every move because they are the baby's sole source of care. Soon, there is the first smile, the first word spoken, and the first step taken. It is only a short time until the child is part of a little league team, learning how to play a sport and what it means to be part of a community. As a teen,

Introduction

they start to discover who they are and what they enjoy doing. They soon reveal who they are to others as they advance through school and get their first job. At some point, they get a sense of their purpose in life and how to be an encouragement and blessing to others. As an adult, they are now making a difference in society and perhaps even becoming a parent. There is plenty in life that is beautiful, noble, and praiseworthy.

At the same time, life is complicated. There is an infinite number of challenges, obstacles, disappointments, trials, physical and emotional ailments, financial stresses, relationship challenges, the death of a spouse, child, or parent, and many other sorrows. Life is undeniably difficult.

Consider the creator. Genesis 1:1 (NLT) says, "In the beginning, God created the heavens and the earth." God also created human beings and desires to have a relationship with that creation. Regrettably, humans chose to disobey God, and their relationship with God broke when they sinned. God is just, and justice requires that there be a punishment for the committed sin. It then became God's plan to have his son Jesus come to the world and die on the cross to suffer the punishment for all the sins committed by the human race. When that happened 2000 years ago, God reconciled to His creation, and we can again have a relationship with God. Can you see the beauty of this plan? It was humans who turned away from God, but it was God who made the sacrifice to win them back.

From the beginning of time to about 100 years after Jesus died on the cross, God's interaction with humans and His message to His creation was recorded. It was first recorded through oral tradition and then written as inspired by God. His message was then organized and compiled into what we now know as the Bible. The Bible reveals God's character to us and is a guide to show us how to live.

Backpacking & the Path of Life

In the same way that we follow a trail when backpacking, the Bible describes a path we can follow in life. Following the backpacking trail is more manageable than bushwhacking but still has obstacles and challenges. The path of life described in the Bible also has its challenges, but when a tree falls while on the path of life, the trail maintainer (God) is there to clear the path or help us overcome the obstacle.

The title of this collection of short stories, *Backpacking & The Path of Life*, is taken from Psalms 16:11 (NIV); "*You make known to me the path of life; you will fill me with joy in your presence, with eternal pleasures at your right hand.*"

God lays out a path for us to follow in life called "the path of life." God reveals the path of life to us through the Bible. The Bible guides us on how to live life while we are here on this planet, and as I am following this path, God "will fill me with joy." This path will ultimately lead us to our eternal life in heaven, where we will have "eternal pleasures."

I described earlier the life cycle of an infant to an adult. When the Bible refers to the path of life, it is so much more than the timeline that transpires from a person's birth to their death. The word "life" describes the quality, vitality, and richness enjoyed through that life cycle. Jesus said in John 10:10 (NIV), "I have come that they may have life, and have it to the full."

As I said before, life is undeniably difficult. When the inevitable tree falls across the path of life, God, in his divine provident nature, determines the best method to maintain the path. He may remove the obstacle and strengthen our faith and trust in him. He may allow the obstacle to remain and help us overcome it instead of removing it. By doing this, He is helping us develop character and perseverance. Regardless of how God is acting on our behalf, He is walking with us on the path of life and will fill us with joy amid the difficulty.

Introduction

Each backpacking story will enhance your own backpacking experience. Whether it is a new trail you add to your bucket list, a new piece of equipment you include in your backpack, or an appreciation of some aspect of life on the trail, I am honored to be part of your backpacking journey.

In addition, I will examine the spiritual parallels in each backpacking story and describe what it would be like to follow the path of life when considering this counterpart. When on the backpacking trail, I am confident you will choose the trail instead of bushwhacking. When making life decisions, I hope this book will help you follow the path of life.

Chapter One

FIRST TIME BACKPACKING

Several teens were leaving the classroom, but the instructors, Jack and Rob, remained. I entered the classroom to see how that night's Rangers class went. The report was good, and soon, the conversation changed. I was the recently hired Children's Pastor for a church in Carlisle, Pennsylvania, and one of my responsibilities was to oversee the Royal Rangers program. Royal Rangers is a scouting-type program with an emphasis on spiritual development. Jack and Rob were the Commanders of the classroom for the oldest group of boys.

Jack probed, "Are you sure you are up to this? It isn't going to be easy." I responded that I was up to the challenge and that this was something I wanted to experience. The truth was that I spent the last 20 years behind a desk in my previous career as an accountant. As a child and teen, I had many outdoor experiences, but hiking 20 miles with a backpack on my back would be a new experience. On top of this was the fact that I was a good 40 pounds overweight. I did want to experience backpacking, but I also saw it as a way to develop relationships with some Ranger leaders. I was in.

Jack gave me some impromptu instructions. "I have a backpack, tent, and sleeping bag you can borrow. You will have to get a good pair of hiking boots, the most important piece of equipment you will wear." Jack also warned that "cotton kills" because it absorbs moisture and can cause hypothermia. Instead, I needed to get synthetic clothing that allows moisture to evaporate. Food must be easy to prepare, light to carry, and high in calories to replenish what the body loses daily.

I spent the next two months putting together what I would wear and carry on my back. I had frequent questions for Jack and Rob as I fine-tuned my equipment. I also started hitting the treadmill to prepare my body for the challenge. The group had grown to five of us: Jack and Rob were the experienced backpackers, while Ranger leaders Dave, Jerry, and myself had never backpacked before. Jack and Rob announced that we would be hiking in the Dolly Sods Wilderness area in West Virginia.

A real sense of anticipation began to build among the Rangers leaders. Everybody was comparing hiking boot prices, food alternatives, and what kind of synthetic clothing was available at Wal-Mart. Over the years, I learned how vital the group energy and planning were to a successful hike. A good hike begins months before the actual event.

Jack had me stop by his house a week before the hike to pick up the equipment I would be borrowing. Having the equipment in advance gave me time to familiarize myself with the backpack and load it with the hiking clothes, supplies, and food I had been collecting. Jack stored his equipment above

First Time Backpacking

his garage, and it felt like I was in an outfitter's store with boxes of supplies, various hanging backpacks, and sleeping bags. He would shuffle through the equipment, stop when he found what he was looking for, pull it off the hook, and then hand it to me. I was thoroughly impressed with his equipment inventory and it showed me how vested he was in his passion of backpacking. His accumulated inventory over the years enabled him to share his passion for backpacking with others.

The day arrived, and it was a four-hour drive to the trailhead, with the last half-hour on a gravel road deep into the mountain. When we arrived, we strapped on our backpacks, and Rob inspected our loads and made some adjustments. We assembled in a circle, and Jack asked the group, "What is your biggest fear about the hike?" Some were afraid of getting lost, others had wisecracks about the body odors of others in the group, while my biggest fear was physical discomforts like blisters or a sprained ankle. Jack led us in prayer, asking God to watch over us as we hiked and hit the trail.

Rob accurately described Dolly Sods as a "playground for hikers." It is not a linear hike, where you park vehicles on two points on the trail and then hike from one car to the other. It is not a loop where you park in one location and then hike in a circle back to the original vehicle. Dolly Sods is a maze of linear trails, loop trails, and connecting trails. There is an endless combination of ways to navigate the wilderness area.

Another unique feature at Dolly Sods is that—instead of marking the trail with paint blazes on the trees—the trails are marked by piles of rocks called "cairns." The word has a Scottish origin and means "heap of stones,"[2] and this method preserves the wilderness beauty of the area.

---

[2] "carin." *Merriam-Webster.com*. 2023. www.merriam-webster.com (February 27, 2023).

Our hike began on a meadow trail that disappeared into a thick forest. My heart was full as we began to hike, and I started singing to myself a camp song I learned as a child.

As we entered the forest, I picked up a stick that became my hiking stick for the rest of the trip. It helped me balance when hopping from rock to rock over creeks. The stick was also handy to push tall grasses off to the side of the trail. Besides all that, I got a real sense of peace from holding onto the stick. It was my security stick.

Our plan for the first day was to hike to a rock outcropping called Lion's Head and then spend the night beneath the pine trees on the summit. This is one of the few hikes I have done that required carrying extra water to where we were spending the night. The standard plan is to camp next to a water source, but an evening on Lion's Head is well worth the extra effort it takes to carry water to the campsite. To get to Lion's Head, take Big Stonecoal Trail to Rocky Point Trail. Travel on Rocky Point Trail for about four-tenths of a mile, where an unmarked path shoots off to the left. There is a small pile of rock cairns to mark the entrance to a path that is very easy to miss. We missed the path.

We were well past the path when we realized we missed it, so we decided to "bushwhack" to the summit. Rob showed us how he oriented where the summit was by finding other physical land features around us that were also on the map. He then used the compass to show us what direction to head. We then began to push our way through chest-high thistles, thorns, rocks, and fallen trees. Avoiding this is why they have trails, and this is why they call it bushwhacking.

Several in the group began to complain, and I wondered why we didn't simply turn around and find the path, but we pushed on. In researching Dolly Sods after this hike, I discovered the military used it in WWII training and that there is

First Time Backpacking

a risk of encountering unexploded bombs.[3] Hiking off of the trail in any area, and especially in Dolly Sods, has a higher level of risk and should be avoided if possible. Hiking off the trail also has a more significant adverse environmental impact on the wilderness.

We finally broke through to the summit to see dozens of mature pine trees and the unmistakable aroma of pine needles. Jack took off running with his arms held straight out like a plane gliding in and out of the pines. The air was thick with enthusiasm; we had arrived!

Jack and Rob helped us set up camp, giving instructions about pitching a tent, making a fire pit, and hanging food. You should ensure there are no rotting branches above where you pitch your tent. It is crucial to clear brush within ten feet of the fire pit. Lastly, ensure you hang your food at least 100 feet from where you are sleeping to keep wild animals away from the tent area.

We spent the next hour or so exploring the summit and taking photos. Rock cairns lead the way to Lion's Head. It doesn't take any imagination to see why they call the outcropping of rocks Lion's Head. It is a 30-foot-tall rock with an obvious jaw, mouth, nose, and eye closely resembling a lion's head.

As the sun set, we returned to camp to prepare dinner. A warm sense of community grew around the campfire. Everyone was curious about what others brought to eat, and there was a little food envy in the air. Rob was dubbed the "Snack Packer" for the variety of snacks he had in his food bag. This name stuck for the remainder of the hike.

After ribbing about who missed the path earlier in the day and chatting about what trails we would hike the next day,

---

[3] "Dolly Sods Wilderness." USDA Forest Service, www.fs.usda.gov/Internet/FSE_DOCUMENTS/stelprdb5090664.pdf. (February 27, 2023).

we headed to our tents for our first night of sleep on the trail. It was April at a higher altitude, with a definite chill. I buried myself in the sleeping bag and shivered for a few minutes before I warmed up and drifted off to sleep.

I woke up several times during the night and had to reposition myself to get comfortable. Ten to twelve hours of sleep is not uncommon on the trail as your body recovers from your previous workout. Getting out of the sleeping bag in the morning took boldness and determination. It was like jumping into cold water. We were back around the campfire for breakfast, with a similar comparison of what everyone was eating. It wasn't long before we were back on the trail heading to Red Rock Creek for our second night of camp.

We made it to Red Rock Creek and went through the same routine of setting up camp and having dinner as we did the previous night. There is a simplicity and rhythm that you experience as you spend several days in the woods. The many complexities of life melt away as your priorities become walking, eating, and sleeping.

We hiked several more trails the following day and then returned to our vehicles to return home. As we exited the forest and began walking on the meadow trail, I realized that I left my hiking stick leaning against a tree when we stopped for a break a mile earlier. It was too far to hike back, but I did consider it. As we pulled away from the trailhead in our vehicles, I studied the fading mountain we had just explored. It is a marvel what lies beneath the treetops: trails and streams, rocks and thistles, rhododendrons and mountain laurels, ridges and cliffs, and a few walking sticks.

The trip back home was filled with talk about our experience and where the next hike would be. There was no doubt in my heart that a passion for backpacking had been born. It became a pursuit of equipment, maps, trail books, and a goal to lose some of the extra body weight I was carrying around. We often develop passions as we journey through life. What I experienced fit me perfectly, and I wanted to experience it more.

> *It is interesting how we develop our passions. We experience something and find it enjoyable. We try it again and have our original experience validated. We research the activity to broaden our knowledge and see that the passion is made even deeper and more meaningful. We don't suddenly acquire a passion for something; it is birthed, nurtured, and grown within us over time. Our passion grows as our relationship with the activity grows.*
>
> *God made us each with different abilities, talents, and personalities, so we all have unique passions. What has become my passion is not necessarily a fit for you. And I am sure there are things you are passionate about that do not fit who I am.*
>
> *There is, however, a passion that is a fit for every human being. Jesus was asked what the greatest commandment is, and his response is recorded in Mark 12:30 (NLT); "And you must love the Lord your God with all your heart, all your soul, all your mind, and all your strength." I am sure you will agree that this sounds like true passion. This love is based on the fact that God sent his son Jesus to take the punishment for my sins by dying on the cross.*
>
> *My sins are forgiven when I believe and accept what Jesus did for me. But Jesus did more than die on the cross; he rose from the dead and showed power*

over death. I can now live free from the guilt of my sins because my sins are forgiven. I will be given eternal life in heaven because of that forgiveness when I die.

Once a person believes and accepts what Jesus did for them, the natural response is to be thankful and joyful. However, having a passion for God and loving God with all your heart is more than just believing that Jesus died on the cross so that your sins can be forgiven. When you accept God's gift of forgiveness, a relationship is birthed between you and God. At this point, God's Holy Spirit comes to live in you, and your body becomes the temple of the Holy Spirit (1 Corinthians 6:19). Meditate on that reality for a moment. Again, God's Holy Spirit comes to live in you. It is a significant event as you move forward on the path of life. Have you encountered an obstacle? God's Holy Spirit is living inside of you to help you navigate around it. Do you need wisdom? God's Holy Spirit is living inside of you to help you make a decision. Are you distraught? God's Holy Spirit is living inside of you to be your comforter.

Let me explain what we believe and know about God— God is part Father, son (Jesus), and Holy Spirit. God is three unique beings in one substance, and all three exist together. God the Father sent His son, Jesus, to earth to die on the cross for our sins. Jesus took our sins upon Himself, died a sacrificial death, and then rose from the dead and returned to God the Father. Then, Jesus sent the Holy Spirit to help us who follow God. God, Jesus, and the Holy Spirit are one God and, at the same time, are three separate and distinct beings.

First Time Backpacking

As I said, when you believe that Jesus died on the cross and rose from the dead and accept the gift of forgiveness that God offers, a relationship is birthed between you and God. That is when his Holy Spirit comes to live in you. This relationship is nurtured and grows when you read the Bible and pray. God can guide you and talk to your heart as you read the Bible. You can talk to God; he can guide and comfort you as you pray. Through this daily and ongoing relationship of reading the Bible and praying, we truly grow to love God with all our hearts, souls, minds, and strength. Our passion grows as our relationship with God grows.

My relationship with God was birthed and nurtured with the help of several faith-filled individuals. As a young teen, I was part of a 4-H Group focused on horse care and riding. The group's leader was Jane Ressler, and the group operated out of her home and horse stable. I would stay at her home over the weekends and sometimes longer, helping with the stable chores and riding school.

On Sundays, I would attend church with Jane's family, and at one service, Jane invited me to go to the altar to pray. At that altar, my relationship with God was birthed when I prayed and asked God to be part of my life. This moment is when I began my journey on the path of life. I remember clearly how that experience left me with a sense of being cleansed and forgiven.

As a 14-year-old, I got my first job as a warehouse worker, where my supervisor was Walt Gouse. Walt talked to me often about the importance of growing in my faith and shared bible-based literature with me to read.

Backpacking & the Path of Life

I drifted away from God as a young adult, got married, graduated from college, and began working as a manager trainee at a lumber yard. One of my co-workers was Jim Kost, who invited my wife and me to attend a church service with his family. At this service, Cindy and I prayed and asked God to be part of our lives.

For Cindy, it was a new experience; it reminded me of what was birthed in me as a teen. We both submerged ourselves in the Bible and prayer and grew to love God with our hearts, souls, minds, and strength. God has been the foundation of our lives through its blessings and challenges. I am so thankful to Jane, Walt, and Jim who were willing to show me the path of life.

Is this all new to you? If so, you can begin following this path of life by simply praying—talking—to God. Speak to God from your heart. Express that you believe in God and his son Jesus, and accept the gift of forgiveness he offers.

I've hiked Dolly Sods several times over the years. It is one of my favorite areas because it is the location of my first backpack trip. I now know how to find the path that leads to Lion's Head, and I no longer have to bushwhack to get there. Now that I think about it, Jack and Rob have both been to Lion's Head several times before our hike. Was missing the turnoff just an excuse to show us how to bushwhack? Oh well, lessons learned.

Chapter Two

TREKKING POLES

Jack, Dave, and I gathered around a folding table in the church gymnasium where our map was laid out. Pointing his finger at a problem stretch, Jack explained why he fondly called it the "Trail of Trials." This particular passage was rocks piled on rocks, typical for Central Pennsylvania. In addition, local landowners often removed markers and felled trees to discourage hikers from using the public access trail. Lastly, there were limited water sources. This trail full of trials was going to be our next challenge.

The actual name of the trail is the Tuscarora Trail. The trail begins in the Shenandoah National Park in Virginia, a blue blaze trail off the Appalachian Trail (AT). The trail ends 250 miles north at the Darlington Shelter, joining up again with the AT in Pennsylvania. The trail was created in the early

1960s out of concern that private landowners were closing sections of the AT, which goes through a more populated area further to the east. If needed, the AT could be rerouted to this western route. The need never materialized as the Appalachian Trail Conservatory was established and began purchasing the corridor needed to ensure a permanent trail further to the east, where it still exists.[4]

The section of the Tuscarora Trail we were going to hike started at Route 233 in Pennsylvania and then joined the AT at the Darlington Shelter. The last leg of our hike would take us on the AT to Boiling Springs. Jack's backyard bordered the AT, and he was a trail maintainer for that section. Our hike would end at Jack's house.

Dave and I had several hikes under our belts, but Jack still took the lead. At this point, I had my own backpack, tent, sleeping bag, white gas stove, and most of the equipment carried by an experienced backpacker. The trail was very physically demanding. There were several steep climbs and descents, and the trail surface was covered with rocks on top of rocks. They were football-sized with just enough surface to place your foot on. You could go for miles, stepping from rock to rock to rock, your feet rarely touching the dirt below.

As had become my tradition, I picked up a hiking stick early on, which helped me balance as I moved from rock to rock. As corny as it sounds, I saved each hiking stick, accumulating them in a corner in my garage. They became souvenirs to remind me of the challenges I faced, the beautiful sights I absorbed, and the friendships I developed while on the trail.

The second day of the hike was the hardest. As Jack warned, local landowners had removed trail markers and

---

[4]Jeff Mitchell, *Backpacking Pennsylvania* (Mechanicsburg, PA: Stackpole Books, 2005), 82.

Trekking Poles

felled trees obscuring visibility. We would wander through the woods, over felled trees, through jaggers, stickers, and brush while looking for trail markers. When we finally made it to the Darlington shelter, we were exhausted. We each prepared our dinner, skipped our normal evening fire, and sunk into our sleeping bags earlier than normal.

The next day, we started our hike on the AT, leading us to Jack's backyard. My knees were incredibly tender and sore, and I was experiencing sharp pains, especially as I hiked downhill. The hiking stick helped relieve the stress on my knees, and I picked up a second stick, now with one for each hand, and experienced even more relief. It then dawned on me—the value of trekking poles! I remember seeing other hikers using trekking poles and would say to myself, "What do they think they are doing? Do they think they are on a ski slope?" As soon as I got home, I started to shop for my first pair of trekking poles.

Trekking poles help you pull yourself up a hill. They also take the stress off your knees as you head down a mountain. Trekking poles help you balance walking from rock to rock, especially when crossing a stream. They are invaluable when traversing a boggy area where you walk on top of logs for an extended stretch. Trekking poles are handy to push brush or tall grasses out of your path. They are even helpful to hold like a sword to clear spider webs when you are the first person on the trail in the morning. I use them to secure my camera for a group selfie, and they can operate as a tent pole for specific tent designs. Lastly, a trekking pole is a perfect place to wrap around an emergency supply of duct tape.

You don't want to go cheap when purchasing trekking poles. One of my backpacking friends fell to the ground as they put all their weight on one of the poles, which snapped. Having collapsible poles to store them easier is nice, but I feel more secure using the flip-style locks than the twist-style ones.

Backpacking & the Path of Life

The hiking stick from the "Trail of Trials" hike was the last stick I kept as a souvenir. A new pair of trekking poles replaced the stick. I have come to depend on my trekking poles. More than anything, they transfer the stress from my knees to the poles, and I no longer hike without them.

In the same way I wouldn't backpack without the aid of trekking poles; I wouldn't walk through life without leaning on God. When life gets difficult, 1 Peter 5:7 (NLT) tells us, "Give all your worries and cares to God, for he cares about you." The picture is for us to give or hand over our worries to God and let him carry our problems. This doesn't mean God is a crutch that eliminates the pain. We are going to experience pain in life, but he will help us carry the anxiety.

This scripture also tells us to give him our worries because he cares about us. Does the creator of the universe actually care about your problem? The degree to which God cares about you is revealed as you read Matthew 10:29-31 (NLT); "What is the price of two sparrows—one copper coin? But not a single sparrow can fall to the ground without your Father knowing it. And the very hairs on your head are all numbered. So don't be afraid; you are more valuable to God than a whole flock of sparrows".

God is not simply a macro manager of the universe who only cares about the "big picture." God cares about the details of life. God cares which of his sparrows has fallen to the ground and how many hairs are on your head. Consider this as you experience wildlife on the trail—God cares about them while He cares about you. Consider this as you encounter problems in life—if God knows how many hairs are on your head, he knows about and cares about your situation. You are loved, and God sees your problems.

Let me describe what giving my worries to God looks like for me. Perhaps you are a student who has a week of final exams, a manager who has an upcoming meeting with a difficult team member, or a parent who needs to talk to a rebellious teen about their behavior. You feel and recognize the anxiety in your heart; it robs you of focus, sleep, and peace. You realize this anxiety is counter-productive, and its presence in your heart makes the challenge you are facing even worse.

Sometimes, I carry the anxiety around longer than I should. Hopefully, sooner rather than later, I get alone with God. I pray and tell God what I am anxious about. I realize He already knows my feelings, but I need to express and articulate them. I will then read some scriptures, perhaps a scripture that has helped me process anxiety in the past. Or maybe a scripture I know has some applicable wisdom or direction, for example, how a Bible character overcame a similar challenge.

Reading the Bible strengthens my faith and reminds me that God has the power to help me face the challenge before me. I pray again, convey what I read in the Bible, and ask him to help me through this challenge. This is how I give my worry to God, and I will often do this several times as God helps me through the situation. Are you anxious about something you will have to face in the future? As you trek on the path of life, you can give that anxiety to God and ask him to carry it for you.

The "Trail of Trials" became a reference point for those of us backpacking together. We would typically describe a trail as "less rocky than the Trail of Trials," "more water than on the Trail of Trials," or "marked better than the Trail of Trials." No one in our group would ever make the mistake of claiming something was in some way harder or more challenging than the "Trail of Trials." Even if it was, admitting it would lessen the shared experience that shaped us as hiking buddies.

Chapter Three
ON OUR OWN

This hike started as a backpacking trip for Jack, Dave, and myself, with Jack as the leader and Dave and I as the students. The destination was the Loyalsock Trail (LT) in Lycoming County, Pennsylvania. This path is a 59-mile linear trail, and we planned to hike it over five days and four nights sometime during October. We did the standard research, which consisted of purchasing maps, reading trail guides, and doing internet research to see what others experienced on the trail. At some point, we compared our calendars and then made the important ask of our spouses.

Once we had a rough plan, we would get more detailed. What time were the sunrise and sunset, so we knew how many hiking hours each day? What were the average nighttime and daytime temperatures so we knew what kind of clothing we would need to pack? Where was the water located, and how far was it from one water source to the next? Where were the campsites located, and did they have water? How would we get to the trailhead, and did we need a shuttle? These were all important questions that would shape the backpacking trip and how we would prepare.

 This trek would be the longest hike that Dave and I had yet experienced. We had done two- and three-night outings, but this would be our first five-day and four-night hike. We invested in all the equipment we were carrying, but now we had to sacrifice some items that we previously thought were necessary to compensate for the fact that this was a longer hike and we needed to carry more food. I loaded my backpack early to see what it weighed, and I was pleased to see I had gotten the weight down to 42 pounds for this five-day hike. Four years later, we did a five-day hike in Maine, and by then, my pack weight was down to 32 pounds. Carrying less weight makes a more enjoyable hike, especially as you age.

 The backpacking trip date was approaching, and our anticipation was climbing as it always does when a trip date gets closer. Then, the news came that Jack had something come up at work and had to bail. Dave and I wondered if we were ready for some of the challenges described in the trail guides. We discussed the prospect of going on the trip without Jack and hesitantly decided to continue with the plan. It was a big step for Dave and me, but we saw it as a challenge we had to tackle.

 As we parked Dave's car at the eastern trailhead, the sun had not yet breached the horizon. Soon, a middle-aged woman pulled up in her badly dented four-door sedan. We piled our packs in her trunk, and for $40, she gave us a thrill ride through the mountain hollows to the western trailhead. Her car reeked with the smell of cigarette smoke, and her rough voice made it clear that she was responsible for the odor. A local hiking club listed her name as a shuttle service. I expected an experienced trail guide, but I doubt she had ever stepped on the trail. We arrived in one piece. Dave and I mounted our packs, asked for God's protection on the hike, and then had our first photo op on the trail.

The trail immediately began to climb from its start at 600 feet to the ridge at 1,900 feet over the first two miles. At this point, Dave and I realized what a challenge we were facing. It was a blend of excitement, anticipation, and a touch of anxiety. I imagine if Jack had been there with us, it would have been about the same except for that touch of anxiety.

Later that day, we reached Smiths Knob Vista and took a break to enjoy some energy bars and trail mix. This vantage point was an exceptional panoramic view of the area we would call home for the next five days.

We started to notice how well this trail was marked. The trail markers were two-inch round, tin-can lids. The lids were painted yellow, with the letters LT hand-painted in red. In addition, every mile had the mileage hand-painted in red instead of the letters LT. It was nice to be able to pace and time our miles. We also started to take a water break every other mile, which was an excellent way to stay hydrated. I returned to the trail recently, and machine-painted plastic discs replaced the tin-can lids. I am sure it is much easier for the local trail club, but I felt a tinge of remorse that the old tradition had faded.

On the first day, we hiked a challenging 13 miles and then set up camp at Hessler Run. After dinner, Dave and I began our nightly ritual of playing 500 Rummy. This game became a staple for all of our future hikes together, and it was not unusual for us to select a campsite based on the rocks available to make a good card table!

The next day, the trail took us through an area rich in history, with buildings still standing that once housed two hotels, each with its own casino and one with two bowling alleys and a dance floor. The fields next to one of the hotels were once a golf course.[5] This area was booming in the late 1800s thanks to the logging industry, and some of the trail used deserted logging roads that traversed throughout the region. We were on a logging road after this historical area when we heard something moving in the woods. As we approached the area, a small black bear dashed onto the trail, ran in front of us for a few yards, and reentered the woods on the opposite side. This sight was a thrill for us and the first bear we saw while backpacking.

The trail guide mentioned that the LT had been rerouted away from Angel Falls to protect it from excessive foot traffic.[6] We hid our backpacks in the weeds and then followed an unmarked path to the base of this 70-foot beauty, one of the tallest waterfalls in Pennsylvania.[7] We explored the falls for over an hour, and it dawned on us how much trouble we would be in if something happened to our hidden backpacks. We rushed back to find that our backpacks safe and continued the hike.

After this 12-mile day, we set up camp on the Kettle Creek Vista. The wind picked up, and it started to rain as we set up our tents. This combination was a new experience for both of us, and it set off a rushed panic, wanting our gear to stay dry as we set up our tents. We ate dinner in our rain gear, skipped the routine campfire and card game, and called it a day.

---

[5]The Alpine Club of Williamsport, *A Guide to the Loyalsock Trail and Side Trails* (15th Revision 2002), 13.
[6]The Alpine Club of Williamsport, *A Guide to the Loyalsock Trail and Side Trails* (15th Revision 2002), 15.
[7]Rusty Glessner. "Road Tripping to the Tallest Waterfalls in PA." PA Bucket List, www.pabucketlist.com/road-tripping-to-the-tallest-waterfalls-in-pa/ (February 27, 2023).

The third day of our trip was filled with water features. We crossed Dutter Run seven times and passed four waterfalls. We had a brief celebration as we encountered the center point of the trail at the 29-mile marker. We then crossed Cape Run twice and Ketchum Run three times. Ketchum Run is also home to Lee Falls and Road Falls. Road Falls had the unique trail feature of a 12-foot wooden ladder to help hikers navigate the steep and rocky terrain. These were all features detailed in the various trail guides we read before our hike. It felt like we were on a tour of God's creation in Pennsylvania. We hiked 15 miles that day and made camp at Double Run.

The fourth day had several stream crossings and waterfalls as we approached World's End Park with its many vistas. It started to rain about midday, and I should have put my rain gear on sooner than I did. Once I put my rain gear on, I felt cold and shivered. I told Dave I was concerned about how chilled I was, and we made our way to a pavilion in the park. I put on some dry clothes, and we waited out the storm. This delay put us behind schedule for the day, and the daylight was starting to fade.

We came to Tom's Run about this time, which would lead us to our planned camping location at Alpine Falls. The fading daylight, a fog settling in the ravine, the moss on the rocks, and the thick woods gave the feel of an enchanted forest. It was indeed one of my all-time favorite experiences on any trail. We made our way to the top of Alpine Falls and set up our camp for the last night of our trip. Despite the wet conditions, Dave got a campfire going, and we enjoyed our last supper in the wilderness overlooking the enchanted forest of Alpine Falls.

Our final day of hiking took us by the Porky Den, which is home to porcupines, Sones Pond, and, lastly, the Haystacks. The Haystacks are an area of large rocks in Loyalsock Creek that do indeed look like haystacks. This led us back to Dave's car, and the hike was done.

> *It would have been great to have Jack as part of this hike, however, at some point, we all need to step out on our own and put into practice what we were taught. This application of knowledge was the model that Jesus used to prepare his disciples as described in Mark 3:14 (NLT); "Then he appointed twelve of them and called them his apostles. They were to accompany him, and he would send them out to preach." This training was a two-step process. First, the disciples spent time with Jesus, where the mentoring occurred. The next step was for Jesus to send the disciples out to preach independently.*
>
> *We should have mentors in our life we learn from and challenge us to grow. I have had several mentors who have challenged me and helped me grow as an individual. This transformation often happens naturally when you are in an organization and those over you take the time to invest in your development. Sometimes, you must be intentional about finding someone you respect and reach out to them for their advice and counsel. This request for help is not a sign of weakness but a sign of maturity, admitting that you need help to grow in an area.*
>
> *Mentors are valuable if you are learning how to backpack, how to be a better parent, or how to succeed in your career. Mentors are even more beneficial if you have a desire to grow spiritually. Whether you have not started your spiritual journey or are a seasoned believer,*

we should all have someone in our life who will challenge us to grow in our relationship with God.

Mentors are not necessarily someone that you have a personal relationship with. There are several authors such as Mark Batterson, John Eldredge, and John Maxwell who have influenced and shaped me as an individual. They have mentored me through their books written and the example they set by how they live. While I am on this topic, I would like to highlight and emphasize the importance and value of reading. I was not always a reader and it wasn't until my mid-thirties that I started to read to expand my fly-fishing knowledge. This reading sparked a hunger for more and other knowledge and my library expanded to books about leadership, personal growth, spiritual growth, American history, world history, social science, and the classics. Charlie "Tremendous" Jones said it best; "You will be the same person in five years as you are today except for the people you meet and the books you read."

In addition to you being mentored, there is very likely someone that God has placed in your life and entrusted you to help them grow. Be open to helping others who reach out to you for help. Meet with them for coffee, listen to their challenges, offer them wise counsel, pray for them, and challenge them to grow like others have challenged you. Having and being a mentor are valuable as you find your way on the path of life.

This journey was an epic hike for Dave and me to experience as our first hike on our own. The trail features were spectacular, but the colorful names given to the various areas and features added to the allure of the region: Pete's Hollow, Peter's Path, Smiths Knob, Painter Run, Snake Run, Big Grand Dad Run, Angel Falls, Springs Window, Mary's View, Split Rock, Lee's Falls, Jack's Window, Winner Nob, Suicide Drop, Worlds End Park, Ken's Window, and of course, my favorite, Alpine Falls.[8]

---

[8]The Alpine Club of Williamsport, A Guide to the Loyalsock Trail and Side Trails (15th Revision 2002), 1.

Chapter Four

ALL FOR ONE

If you live in Pennsylvania and are interested in outdoor activities, you probably heard of what the locals call the Little Grand Canyon. I've seen its namesake in Arizona, and there really is no comparison between these two land features. Any backpacker in Pennsylvania is naturally drawn to this area of the state. Pine Creek created the Little Grand Canyon and has the West Rim Trail on the northern end.[9] Further south on Pine Creek is the Black Forest Trail. On the top of the mountain is the Sentiero Di Shey Trail, and throughout the area many other connecting trails enable you to make a trek longer or shorter if needed.

---

[9] Chuck Dillon, *Guide to the West Rim Trail* (Wellsboro, PA: Pine Creek Press, 1999), 6.

As a new backpacker, I began researching the trails in this area and decided to hike the West Rim Trail. I ordered the maps and trail guide from Pine Creek Outfitters and then laid out my plan for my hiking buddies, Jack and Dave. They were both on board without any hesitation. We headed to the shop on a Monday morning early in November. We completed the required camping permit, and then the outfitter drove us to the southern trailhead, where we would begin our hike. We would hike north on the 30-mile trail back to our parked car at the northern trailhead.

The West Rim Trail is a well-maintained trail with a good supply of water and many vistas. It is a moderately difficult trail that goes out of its way to avoid steep climbs and descents. We spent our first night at a vista after a 12-mile day of hiking. A large flat rock was next to the fire pit, which served as a kitchen counter as we prepared our dinner and as a card table for our customary game of 500 Rummy. With the sun setting early this time of year, we headed to our tents and got our regular ten-plus hours of sleep.

We woke to an unusual view of the gorge, which had filled with a thick, puffy fog during the night. It was indeed a beautiful sight! I alluded earlier to the fact that you can't compare the land features of the Little Grand Canyon to its namesake in the West. This comment does not mean one is inferior or not as beautiful as the other. They are too different to be compared.

They each have their unique beauty. The American West has a vast, dramatic, and majestic landscape. The East has a vibrant, growing, and earthy landscape. To one person, the cliffs, raging rivers, and glacier lakes are superior. To another person, the moss-covered forest floor, trickling mountain streams, and rhododendron-covered hillsides are superior. They are all fantastic creations of an amazing God and without comparison.

Tuesday's terrain was similar to the previous day's hike, with easy trails, plenty of water, and several vistas. There was no pressure to conquer the trail—as on some hikes—so we were more relaxed than usual. We began taking extended breaks and naps at each vista. We would drop our packs, unroll our ground pads, nap a little, and enjoy the scenery for a while. We spent our second night along the Right Branch of the Four Mile Run after a 12-mile day of hiking. This schedule would leave us a little over six miles of hiking on the last day. We referred to doing fewer miles on the final day as an "easy- out." We try to hike enough miles in the first few days of a hike so that the last day has fewer miles, which makes the drive home more manageable. This day was supposed to be another "easy out."

We woke up the following day to a drizzle, quickly broke camp, and put on our rain gear. As we started to hike, I realized that something was wrong. I started feeling nauseous and got sick at several points along the trail. I had several other virus-like symptoms, such as a headache, high fever, and stomach cramps. The worst part was that I had zero energy. It was an effort to move on the trail even at a very slow pace. We were all concerned, and I had no idea the cause of this sudden illness. I speculated that it was food poisoning, bad water, or some virus, but I didn't know. Jack and Dave could see my condition and, without my knowledge, called the outfitters and had them pick us up where the trail crossed Colton Road, about four miles short of our final destination.

When you are on the trail and things are not going according to plan, these are the kind of friends that you need! King Solomon's words are recorded in Ecclesiastes 4:12 (NLT): 'A person standing alone can be attacked and defeated, but two can stand back-to-back and conquer. Three are even better, for a triple-braided cord is not easily broken.' The concept is clear: It is better to do life with the help of others. Doing life together is one of the great reasons to be a part of a church. It's how life was meant to be when you follow Jesus. This scripture reinforces the value of being part of a church.

Some argue that you can follow God without being part of a church. While our salvation is not dependent on attending church, the Bible tells us that God wants us to. Paul encourages us to meet together. In Hebrews 10:25 (NLT), he says, 'And let us not neglect our meeting together, as some people do.'

We are each created with unique gifts, talents, and abilities, and the church is incomplete if all its members are not participating. Just like I needed Jack and Dave's help while on the trail, the church community is there to help each other as they do life together.

One function of the church is to equip you to serve others. Whether it is serving by welcoming others into the church, helping to clean or maintain the church building, or being part of a food bank, serving others is integral to your spiritual growth (Ephesians 4:11-16). Serving helps others just like Jack and Dave helped me, but you are also growing as an individual as you serve. Serving helps us to focus on others instead of focusing on ourselves.

Church is where we assemble to worship God and celebrate what God has done for us. We remember what Jesus did for us on the cross through the ceremony of Holy Communion. We publicly announce our belief in Jesus through water baptism.

Since the church is made up of humans and since every human is flawed, it is inevitable that there will be some level of conflict. Regardless, this is not a valid excuse for not being part of a church. Difficulties shape you and others and help us become more spiritually mature. If you have begun your journey on the path of life, you need to be part of a church.

There is excellent value in hiking with other people instead of hiking solo. The ideal number is four because if one is injured, one can stay with the injured person, and the other two can go for help. As a group, you should always let the weakest person become the standard for how the rest of the group proceeds.

Several years after my West Rim Trail trip, I was hiking with a group of four in the Smoky Mountains. It was me, my co-workers, Denny and Tom, and Tom's son Trent, on a four-day hike in May. We had the required Smoky Mountain backcountry permits, and I put together a 26-mile loop that started at the Crosby Campground in Tennessee and then linked together the Gables Mountain Trail, Maddron Bald Trail, Snake Den Ridge Trail, Appalachian Trail, Camel Gap Trail, and Low Gap Trail, which led back to the Crosby Campground. Our daily mileage was five miles on Thursday, seven on Friday, nine on Saturday, and five on Sunday. We would be camping where Greenbrier Creek crosses Gables Mountain Trail on night one, Otter Creek crosses Maddron Bald Trail on night two, and Big Creek runs next to Camel Gap Trail on night three.

Much of the Smoky Mountain area was previously inhabited by mountain communities that had been abandoned when the National Park was created.[10] It is an area rich in early

---

[10] Michael Joseph Oswald, *Your Guide to the National Parks* (Whitelaw, WI: Stone Road Press, 2022), 109.

American history and natural beauty. What struck me about the area's ecology were the number of mountain streams and the moisture content in the air and soil. It felt like we were in a rainforest, and the size of the trees was impressive. There was an abundance of wildflowers, mushrooms, and small wildlife such as snails and salamanders. It is truly a national treasure and a fantastic area to backpack.

From the beginning of the hike, Trent complained of feeling sluggish and lacking energy. Trent was in his twenties, had served our country in the military, and was always full of energy and enthusiasm on past hikes that he had done with us. He used his canvas military-issue backpack, filled it completely, and probably carried twice the weight on his back as we did. It was not unusual for Trent to sneak off the trail while we were hiking and hide in the woods ahead of us, making bird calls as we approached. It was evident that Trent was struggling and was not himself on this hike.

On Saturday, the third day of the hike, we came to an intersection where the Maddron Bald Trail ran into the Snake Den Ridge Trail. We were to continue on the Snake Den Ridge Trail to the right for an additional seven miles of hiking on Saturday and then five miles on Sunday to complete the loop. To the left, the Snake Den Ridge Trail was a four-mile hike back to Crosby Campground, where the SUV was parked.

I pulled out the map and proposed cutting the hike short because of Trent's challenges. Denny said he would hike with Trent back to the SUV and let Tom and I finish the planned hike. All agreed that this would work, and the group split in two. Denny and Trent hiked the four miles back to the Crosby Campground. Tom and I camped as planned at Big Creek on Saturday night and then finished the loop on Sunday. By this time, Trent and Denny had showered at the campground and had pizza for dinner. Trent was feeling better and thankful that he could get off the trail a little early. Because there were four of us on this hike, we were able to change our hike plans and accommodate Trent's situation.

In the case of Jack, Dave, and myself, when we were hiking on the West Rim Trail earlier in this chapter, we quickly made it back to our car with the help of the outfitter and began the journey home. I never did figure out the cause of my sudden sickness, but I do know that the concept of the "easy out" took on new significance as we did the last four miles of the hike in the backseat of the outfitter's SUV. On that hike and this one, the Bible's wisdom is true — life is much easier to navigate when you have the help of others!

Chapter Five

A CHANGE OF PLANS

I enjoy the planning aspect of backpacking. Whether it's a hike on the Appalachian Trail, which has multiple access points within a few miles of where I live, or a flight out west to hike in a National Park, I can over-plan like no one else! What section of the trail are we hiking? How are we going to get there and then return home? Are permits required for camping? What will the weather "likely" be, and how will that impact what we carry on our backs? What is the availability of water and camping sites on the trail? Are bear canisters required for your food? Is carrying bear spray recommended? A well-planned hike is a safer hike.

Several years into my passion for backpacking, I began inviting friends, co-workers, and family members to go with me. Sometimes, those I took had little or no experience backpacking. Planning became even more critical because I had to plan not only for myself, but for the safety and enjoyment of the hike by others.

One such backpacking companion was Butch. Butch and I were on staff together at the same church in Carlisle, Pennsylvania. I was the Children's Pastor, responsible for youngsters from the crib to grade six. Butch was the Youth Pastor and had the responsibility for young people in grades seven through twelve. We were both working many hours and needing a getaway to refresh. After some research, we decided to hike the Black Forest Trail in the Tiadaghton State Forest in Pennsylvania. This trail is a 43-mile loop categorized as a strenuous hike.[11] Many water features and vistas make it beautiful and challenging. Various side trails enable you to make it a shorter or longer hike if needed.

This was not Butch's first hike. As he began to accumulate his gear, I supplemented some of the things he had not yet acquired. One item I supplied was his rain gear. Rain gear is one of those items that you can find other substitutes for until you have the bucks to get the higher-end versions. Breathability is the most vital quality to look for in rain gear. PVC rain gear keeps out the rain but holds in your body heat, so you get wet, not by the rain, but by your sweat.

Breathable rain gear has pores that let your body's heat escape but miraculously keeps out the rain. The problem with breathable rain gear is how expensive it is and that's why it is one of the last items many backpackers purchase. I purchased a lower-end breathable rain suit, but it was heavy. When I

---

[11]Jeff Mitchell, *Backpacking Pennsylvania* (Mechanicsburg PA: Stackpole Books, 2005), 138.

A Change of Plans

upgraded my equipment, I bought a lightweight version that was a third of the weight. I let Butch borrow my heavier rain suit for this hike.

The day had arrived, and we headed to the trailhead in Slate Run, PA. We were about one mile into the hike when we had to cross over Slate Run. Slate Run is a medium-sized mountain creek with a pretty good flow. I looked for an easy crossing but couldn't find one, so I removed my boots and socks, put on my sandals, rolled up my pant legs, and quickly navigated my way across the stream.

Butch didn't want to be hassled with removing his boots and proceeded to pick his way across the stream from rock to rock. He almost made it when he lost his footing and fell backward into the creek. His backpack was submerged in the water, and after much flailing of his arms and legs, he made it to the other side. It was evident that this was going to detour our plans, but when I saw blood flowing from his upper lip, we realized that the trip might be totally in jeopardy. As Butch was flailing his arms around to catch his balance, one of his trekking poles cut into his upper lip.

Butch was devastated and kept repeating how he had ruined our hike. I had concerns as well but was not ready to give up. We returned to the trailhead, and I drove Butch to the Wellsboro Hospital, which was a 45-minute drive away. I dropped Butch off at the emergency room and headed to a laundromat in Wellsboro with Butch's equipment. I dried his gear and returned to the hospital to pick him up. Butch now had a big lip with stitches and, thanks to the laundromat, dry gear. We went back to the trailhead and started again. This time, we both removed our shoes and socks and rolled up our pants legs to cross Slate Run. Despite the four-hour delay, we arrived at our originally planned campsite for the night.

Backpacking & the Path of Life

The next morning was overcast when we started hiking, but it soon turned into a significant downpour. We put on our rain gear and plodded on. Hiking in the rain is never pleasant, but it can be done. You first drop your backpack and pull out your rain suit. Hopefully, you packed it close to the top of your backpack so it is easy to get to. You put your rain suit on and leave as many of its vents and openings unzipped as possible to let your body heat escape. Even with the best rain suit, it will trap some of your body heat, and you will begin to sweat. You then cover your backpack with your waterproof backpack cover. Most backpacks are not waterproof, and you need a cover that is readily available in case it starts raining. I keep my backpack cover in the top lid of my backpack. You then hike on, adjusting the vents and zippers to let your body heat escape and keep out the rain.

It wasn't long before Butch was complaining about how wet he was. I assumed it was just from his body sweat, but when he showed me how wet his shirt was under his (my) rain gear, it was evident it had failed. The rain gear had served me well but was ready to be replaced. We came upon a mountain cabin with a five-foot by eight-foot porch and set up camp there. Butch changed out of his wet clothes and into some dry ones, and we heated some water for hot coffee. We ended up being on that porch for the next 24 hours. There was not a topic or world problem that we did not discuss during that time. In reflection, this was probably the highlight of the hike. Not that it was such a bad hike, but that it gave Butch and me the chance to get to know each other better.

We had to modify the remainder of our hike because of our day on the porch. Fortunately, we were able to get off the Black Forest Trail on a side trail so that we could be back home as expected. This hike taught me two important lessons. First, having good equipment can make the difference between finishing a hike according to plan or sitting on a porch for a day. More importantly, you must remain flexible and not let your plan dictate your hike. It is more important to let the hike dictate your plan. Plans need to change when someone's health or safety becomes a concern. You plan for what is likely to happen but embrace the unexpected.

I have seen this play out on many backpacking trips. You have a good plan, but something unexpected happens, and everyone gathers around the map. You discuss the risks of moving forward with the original plan and the alternate plans that could be made. You consider those in the group and how staying the course or changing the plan will impact the other hikers. Then, you pray, ask God for wisdom, and change the plan. I enjoy being able to change the plan on the fly as much as I enjoy creating a good plan in the first place.

> *I would be leaving out an important part of the planning process if I didn't share King Solomon's words recorded in Proverbs 16:3 (NLT): "Commit your actions to the Lord, and your plans will succeed." The need for planning permeates every aspect of life. Inviting God to be part of your plan is crucial to its success in life and while on the trail. At the same time, we need to do our part and use the brains that God gave us as we plan.*

> *You may find your job unfulfilling, and you know that you need to make a change. Your plan for change should start with a prayer to God, asking him to guide you as you consider a new career. You begin to research what the new career might be. This may involve taking a personality test or gifts survey to see what type of job might fit you best. You would also research what jobs are available in the marketplace that would suit you. All*

along, you have included God in the process as you go to him in prayer daily. You are committing the plan to God, and when you do this, Proverbs 16:3 tells you that you will succeed. You are not depending on yourself for the best outcome but trusting in God to lead you. This process is not meant to sound like an item on a simple list of things to do so that you can check it off your list.

Pray ✓
Commit your plans to God ✓
Success ✓

You should approach plans and decisions such as this humbly and sincerely. You should examine your desires and motives to ensure they align with godly principles. With this mindset, your success is defined as God's desires or His will being accomplished in your life.

I can say emphatically that you should commit your plans to God. The result will not necessarily be what you expect it to be or think it should be. What if your desired outcome for this plan contradicts God's will for your life? Indeed, you want God's will to prevail. Here is where your faith intersects with your plan. You will commit your plan to God and do your best to follow His leading. As the results unfold, you will continue to trust Him, no matter what the outcome, knowing that you have committed this plan to Him. With an attitude such as this, you will succeed!

You have done all your research, applied at several companies, and were just offered a new position. Your prayer will now be to ask God to confirm in your heart where your plan has taken you. Throughout this process, God has guided you, not through an audible voice,

A Change of Plans

but through the Holy Spirit within you. This is not a physical voice but a still, small voice that you will learn to recognize as you mature as a believer.

In addition to seeking God for a specific need each morning, you should ask him to guide your steps for the day ahead. Your plans must be flexible enough to allow God to change them to accomplish his mission. We never know when listening to God in this manner will keep us from harm or enable us to be a blessing to someone else during our day. Committing your plans to God is crucial as you follow the path of life.

Like all hikes this particular one had its challenges; but the area is beautiful and it was awesome getting to know Butch better. I have many fond memories of this hike, but none beat the sight of Butch taking his shoes and socks off and rolling up his pant legs as we re-crossed Slate Run the second time!

Chapter Six

BACKPACKING WITH CINDY

It was never easy for my wife, Cindy, when I would disappear into the woods for a few days with my hiking buddies to do a backpacking trip. She would worry a little and say, "Don't get lost. Please don't overdo it. Watch out for snakes, and watch the weather for bad storms." I would reassure her that I would be fine and leave her behind to hold the family together and handle things if anything urgent surfaced. Jack and Dave had similar circumstances, and we came up with the idea to have a couple's hike so that our wives could experience what we had come to enjoy so much.

I promised Cindy that we would find a section of trail that was flat and easy to hike, and I assured Cindy that I had never seen anything other than a harmless garter snake on the trail. She was in, as was Jack's wife Carol and Dave's wife Laura.

Our first step was to get Cindy hiking boots and clothes, which was easy because Cindy is always game to shop for clothes. When I purchased my first backpacking tent, I intentionally bought a two-person version for the added space it offered. I also knew that—at some point—I wanted to take Cindy backpacking, so I purchased a matching set of lightweight sleeping bags that we connected to make one large bag. Lastly, I borrowed a backpack and trekking poles from Jack for Cindy.

We chose an 11-mile section of the Appalachian Trail (AT) from Shippensburg Road to Caledonia State Park. This would be a two-day hike in September, a beautiful time to be outdoors in Pennsylvania. We did the necessary vehicle shuttle and were on our way. It was great to see Cindy with her backpack on and trekking poles in hand. It meant a lot to us to have our wives as part of this hike.

We soon crossed over Birch Run and were on our way to our camping site for the night when we saw what looked like a pile of small rocks on the trail in the distance. It turned out to be a huge rattlesnake coiled up in the center of the trail. Up to this point in my life, I had spent much time in the woods—horseback riding, fishing, and now backpacking—and I had never seen a rattlesnake in the wild. I couldn't believe this rattlesnake appeared when I was with Cindy, who was so freaked out by snakes! We chased it off the trail, with Cindy handling it pretty well, and now we could both say that we saw a rattlesnake in the wild.

We set up camp near Long Pine Run, where we could get water after our four-mile hike. It was a different role for me, setting up our temporary home and then cooking dinner for Cindy, and she enjoyed the break from the usual routine. We made a campfire, which took the chill out of the air, and we had a great time interacting with my hiking buddies and their wives. We headed to our tents for the night, and it wasn't long before Cindy observed the many sounds in the woods at night: crickets chirping, frogs croaking, owls howling, and trees creaking. It is music to my ears, but for Cindy, it prompted the question: what is out there that she can't hear? I brought earplugs to protect Cindy from my snoring, but they also worked well to help her block out the unseen creators of the beautiful music of the forest.

Our second day would involve a seven-mile hike to the car we had parked at Caledonia State Park. Jack did a fantastic job finding a local trail stretch with few elevation changes and a smooth surface. We had lunch at Quarry Gap Shelter and then hiked through a beautiful tunnel of rhododendrons. Suddenly, as Cindy was gazing around at the area's beauty, she took a misstep, turning her ankle and falling to the ground.

We helped her up, and it was clear she was in a lot of pain. Dave took her backpack, and I gave her a shoulder to lean on for the rest of the hike. We were only about a mile from the car, but unfortunately, it was a 500-foot rock-covered descent to Caledonia State Park. The next day, an x-ray revealed a crack in her fibula bone, and she had to wear a cast for the next six weeks. I was Cindy's servant until the ankle healed and the cast was removed!

Despite the rattlesnake, forest music, and broken ankle, Cindy enjoyed the backpacking experience and said she wanted to do it again. I got Cindy her own backpack and trekking poles for Christmas, and I began to look for our next hike. My research took me to the Sentiero Di Shay Trail, a 13-mile loop in the Tiadaghton State Forest of Pennsylvania. The trail is a deserted railroad bed used for logging, accounting for its level surface. The trail is mostly at higher elevations and not far from the area known as Pennsylvania's Little Grand Canyon.

I didn't want to take Cindy hiking on a trail I didn't know firsthand, so I decided to hike it in advance without her. I also wanted to avoid bothering my hiking buddies with such an easy trail, so I decided to hike the trail solo. There is a little higher risk in solo hiking, and you have to plan accordingly. Let others know where you plan to hike and your itinerary, so if you don't return when expected, others will know where to look for you.

Getting lost on a well-marked trail is unlikely, but you could have a physical injury that would leave you stranded and waiting for help. My assessment is that the most dangerous part of backpacking is gathering firewood for the evening campfire. You are now off the trail and climbing through brush, fallen trees, and rocky mounds to find the trophy piece of sun-dried hardwood. There is a much greater risk of encountering wildlife or twisting an ankle when gathering firewood, and you need to be careful when you go off the trail—especially when you are solo hiking.

It was later in March, and this solo hike would be my first for the year. It always feels great to return to the woods once winter has passed. There were still piles of snow in the parking area, and the buds were not yet on the trees. I planned to hike the ten miles to where the Sentiero Di Shay Trail and the Black Forest Trail intersect and set up camp next to the County Line Stream. This plan would leave me an easy three-mile hike back to my car the next morning.

Solo backpacking does have a different feel to it. The actual hiking part is about the same; you are often alone in your thoughts, whether hiking with a group or on your own. The real difference is when you are at camp for the night. I missed the interaction with others when preparing and eating meals and the general poking fun and banter that happens around the campfire.

I had to push myself to gather firewood and build a fire, knowing I would be the only one to enjoy it. Still, I made the effort and was glad I did. There was a quiet calm as I gazed into the flames, realizing it would be better if others were there to enjoy it with me. I was also glad I ventured out to do a solo hike. I had a sense of accomplishment, knowing that I had my first backpacking experience just a few years earlier and was now doing this on my own. With nothing else to do, I headed to bed early with the satisfaction of experiencing my first solo hike.

The next morning, I packed up camp and quickly returned to my car for the ride home. I now knew first hand that Cindy could hike this trail. Cindy and I planned to hike the Sentiero Di Shay Trail just two months later, in May.

May arrived and seeing the transformation that occurred in the woods in the short two months was awesome. The piles of snow were gone in the parking lot, ferns bordered the trail, and the trees were now in full bloom. We planned to hike the eight miles to a campsite on the headwaters of the Francis Branch Creek. We were about halfway to our destination when we heard the faint rumble of thunder. I had checked the weather forecast in advance, as I always do before a hike, and there was nothing on the radar that looked threatening.

But we were in the mountains, and pop-up storms do happen, and that is why I always carry rain gear just in case. This is nothing out of the ordinary to a seasoned backpacker, but I had hoped this hike would be uneventful. As you may recall, our first trip had the drama of a rattlesnake coiled up on the path, and then, near the end of the journey, Cindy broke her ankle. I began to pray for the storm to turn and miss us. My prayer was unanswered, and we started putting on our rain gear.

You know when you are about to be hit by a storm. The wind picks up, there is a sudden temperature change, and the leaves on the trees flip over. I remember Rob telling me on my first hike that the tree leaves flipping over are caused by a sudden increase in humidity. The leaf stem becomes limp, and the breeze flips the leaf over so that the underside of the leaf is now pointed towards the sky. This happening is a reliable sign that you are about to get wet. By this time, the storm was imminent; we could see lightning flashes, and thunder cracks immediately followed them.

I don't say this to make the situation sound more dramatic than it was, but the truth is, it became the most severe lightning storm I ever experienced on the trail up to that point or since. Why now, with Cindy only on her second hike? You don't want to be the tallest object in the woods during a lightning storm, and you don't want to stand at the base of the tallest object because the lightning can follow the object to its base.[12] We leaned our aluminum trekking poles at the base of a tree, kneeled in the center of the trail, and waited out the storm. Cindy handled the rage of the storm in the same calm manner she dealt with the rattlesnake and broken ankle, and I couldn't help but be impressed.

> *Most of what we worry about never materializes. In Cindy's case, her fear of snakes, injury, and storms all happened. Regardless, Matthew 6:25-34 (NLT) cautions us against worry; "That is why I tell you not to worry about everyday life—whether you have enough food and drink, or enough clothes to wear. Isn't life more than food, and your body more than clothing? Look at the birds. They don't plant or harvest or store food in barns, for your heavenly Father feeds them. And aren't you far more valuable to him than they are?*

---

[12]Amy Rost, *Survival Wisdom & Know-How* (New York, NY: Black Dog and Leventhal Publishers, 2007), 638.

Can all your worries add a single moment to your life? And why worry about your clothing? Look at the lilies of the field and how they grow. They don't work or make their clothing, yet Solomon in all his glory was not dressed as beautifully as they are. And if God cares so wonderfully for wildflowers that are here today and thrown into the fire tomorrow, he will certainly care for you. Why do you have so little faith? So don't worry about these things, saying,' What will we eat? What will we drink? What will we wear?' These things dominate the thoughts of unbelievers, but your heavenly Father already knows all your needs. Seek the Kingdom of God above all else, and live righteously, and he will give you everything you need. So don't worry about tomorrow, for tomorrow will bring its own worries. Today's trouble is enough for today.".

God will meet your needs and take care of the birds that cross your path on the trail and the wildflowers in the meadow where you camp. Worrying doesn't lessen the problem, but the distraction caused by worrying could make the situation worse. For example, not being able to sleep because you are worried about a management meeting you have at work the next day could keep you from thinking clearly at the meeting.

Worry or fear is the opposite of faith. Having faith is essential, and Hebrews 11:6-7 (NLT) tells us, "It is impossible to please God without faith. Anyone who wants to come to him must believe that God exists and that he rewards those who sincerely seek him." Our faith in God was demonstrated when we first believed that God exists. You never saw God face to face, so it takes faith to believe he exists. This act of faith so pleased God that he forgave your sins. God is equally pleased when you have faith in him to help you with your worries.

When we worry, it's often because we are focused on our problems rather than God and his amazing love and provision. We may even momentarily forget that God is able and ready to help us. God can help you; after all, he created the entire universe. God is prepared to help you, which became evident when he sent Jesus to die for your sins.

If you worry about something, remember that God is walking with you on the path of life, and if what you fear does happen, God is beside you to help you through it.

We hiked the remaining few miles to a campsite I had scouted two months earlier, and then we set up camp. By this point, the storm was a distant memory, and the air was fresh and clean, as it usually is after a gully washer of a storm. The storm left the creek higher adding to this campsite's beauty. If there were a rating service for campsites, this would be a five-star site.

Not every campsite is ideal. Sometimes, as daylight diminishes, you compromise your standards and set up camp on a weed-infested hillside. Once, when a storm approached, I set up camp on the trail. More than once, I set up camp on the porch of a cabin when it was too wet and rainy to pass up the convenience of a dry porch. You know a five-star site when you see one. There is always a stream with good water flow to fill your water bottles, rinse your coffee cup, and take a quick sponge bath. There is, of course, a nice firepit with logs placed around it for seating. The site is used just enough to keep the weeds down but not overused to the point of depleting all of the firewood. There are several cleared areas to pitch your tent, and the ground is soft enough to insert a tent spike easily. Pine needles are dusted throughout the site, giving a cushioned walking surface and a sweet pine-scented aroma. This site had a stone mound topped with a large flat rock to provide a place to prepare dinner—this was a very nice touch!

We set up camp, hung our wet clothes out to dry, and I prepared supper. Cindy again told me how much she appreciated me taking care of our meals and setting up our temporary home, and it made me wonder if I should do this once in a while when we got back home. I packed some marshmallows for dessert that I toasted over the campfire, and then we enjoyed the fire before heading to the tent for the night. The stream water flow provided some white noise that drowned out the music of the forest, and we drifted off to sleep.

We woke to the sounds of the stream in the morning. I prepared breakfast and we packed up camp and mounted our backpacks. As I usually do before I hit the trail in the morning, I prayed and asked for God's protection while on the trail. I don't know if Cindy noticed, but I got choked up as I considered God's faithfulness on the trail. Despite the past challenges of the rattlesnake, the broken ankle, and the violent lightning storm, God took care of us and provided me with a wonderful wife who would subject herself to this backpacking hobby that had become such a passion for me. God is good!

Chapter Seven

HUNDRED-MILE WILDERNESS

The name "Hundred-Mile Wilderness" invokes a sense of adventure and mystery. The Hundred-Mile Wilderness is the longest remote section of the Appalachian Trail (AT). This section adds the challenge of no supply points from Monson to Baxter Park in Maine.[13] At the conclusion of the Hundred-Mile Wilderness is the final destination point of Mount Katahdin. Not only is it notable for its remoteness and length, but it also boasts some of the trail's most challenging and beautiful landscapes. It is poetic for those who start hiking at Springer Mountain in Georgia, then hike for the next six months, to arrive at a final epic stretch of 100 miles and then climb hand

---

[13]Ray Ronan, *The Appalachian Trail Guide to Maine* (Augusta, MA: Maine Appalachian Trail Club, 2004), 42, 59.

over hand up the face of Mount Katahdin before reaching the summit. The drama and crescendo created by this final part of their journey are well-documented by those "thru-hikers" who have experienced it.

The AT begins at Springer Mountain in Georgia and treks northward to Maine for more than 2,150 miles. The AT provides an excellent recreation opportunity for hikers in the 14 states it passes through. The AT is also used by "thru-hikers" whose goal is to hike from Springer Mountain in Georgia to Mount Katahdin in Maine as a continuous journey. Thousands of hikers attempt a thru-hike each year, with only about one in four completing the journey successfully. A typical thru-hiker will start in Georgia in March and then follow the emergence of spring and summer through the middle states, completing the hike before winter in Maine.[14] I greatly respect and admire those who set out to thru-hike the AT, and I have a sense of awe for those who complete it. These determined individuals show excellent physical and mental stamina to overcome the challenges of hiking the long distance. They endure the wear and tear on their bodies, persevere through adverse weather conditions, and forego the comforts of modern society for nearly half a year. While I have hiked various parts of the trail in four states, my experience is far from what these thru-hikers have accomplished.

My research for hiking in the Hundred-Mile Wilderness began with a call to Shaw's Hiker Hostel in Monson, Maine. I called in the spring and was told they still had several feet of snowpack. A spring hike was obviously not an option. They warned of the black flies in the summer and the fact that snow can shut down the trail again in November. Early October

---

[14]Bill Bryson, *A Walk in the Woods, Rediscovering America on the Appalachian Trail* (NY, NY: Broadway Books, 1998), 7.

would be an excellent time to make a backpacking trip. I knew the entire 100-mile hike would be more than I could handle, and I was glad to hear they had a shuttle service to Jo-Mary Road. They could drop us off at this point, and then we could hike the 58 miles back to our vehicle, which would be parked at a trailhead on Route 15 outside of Monson.

I anxiously waited for the map and trail guide I ordered, and once they arrived, I spread them out and began to see what a hike in this 58-mile section would look like. How far was it between each shelter? Was there water at each shelter and at points between each shelter? What would the daily elevation changes be, and were there other challenges like stream crossings or rock climbs? How many daylight hiking hours would there be, and what would the temperature range be? I tried many different configurations and settled on what I thought would be the best approach to tackle the 58-mile section. It would take five days of hiking, with daily miles being fifteen, thirteen, eleven, nine, and ten. I was concerned with the number of climbs and descents required daily and questioned whether the hike was beyond our capabilities.

I met with Jack, Dave, and Butch to show them the trail map and to roll out my plan for the five-day hike. Everyone had the same concerns about the number of steep climbs and descents and the remoteness of the area we would be backpacking. This hike was well beyond what any of us had previously attempted. These were all healthy concerns, but the allure of hiking the Hundred-Mile Wilderness won out, and the four of us would sign up for this adventure. Over the next several months, we did additional research about backpacking this section of the trail. We also looked for ways to eliminate pack weight to carry the extra food required for a five-day hike.

The big day in October had arrived, and we headed 12 hours north to Shaw's Hiker Hostel on a Monday. Jack drove his crew cab pickup, and as typical, he drove the distance as if he were in a race. According to Jack, we won.

We paid our fee for beds in the bunkhouse and then mingled with the rest of the hikers to discover that most were thru-hikers getting ready to do the last leg of their 2,150-mile journey. I was amazed at the diversity of the group. One fellow in his mid-50s was recently divorced, and this was his way of resetting his life. He was in a constant state of agitation, and we kept our distance. A retired couple was doing the thru-hike, and while their attitudes were very positive, it was obvious that their bodies were worn out from the journey with both having bandages around various body parts. Several college-age hikers were energetic and excited about the last part of their journey.

Although these individuals hiked independently of each other, they all seemed to know each other. You might get more information about hikers when someone else speaks about them than when they talk to you. I was also struck by their rough appearance. After all, they had lived in the woods for the past six months, and personal hygiene had ceased to be a priority.

Tuesday began with a breakfast buffet provided by Shaw's, and this was a real treat, knowing that we would be spending the next five days in the wilderness. We were then shuttled to drop off Jack's truck on Route 15 outside of Monson and shuttled to Jo-Mary Road to begin hiking. The shuttle driver took a group photo of us with one of our cameras, and we were then on our way. We passed Church Pond and Crawford Pond and climbed Little Boardman Mountain. We then descended to cross the East Branch of the Pleasant River and began our climb up White Cap Mountain.

Our destination for the night was Logan Brook Shelter, which is about halfway up White Cap Mountain. We steadily climbed throughout the day, starting at Jo-Mary Road at an elevation of 800 feet to the Logan Brook Shelter at an elevation of 2,400 feet. This was a climb of 1,600 feet over a 15-mile distance. As Pennsylvania hikers, we were used to climbing 2,000-foot mountains that started at 1,000 feet. So, a climb of 1,000 feet in Pennsylvania was considered a challenge. This was a much higher climb over a 15-mile day, so we were pretty well spent. We had the shelter to ourselves and were pleased to have this long day of hiking behind us.

We heard about the prolific mouse population in Maine, and this shelter, as well as the other shelters, had much evidence of mouse activity and mouse traps. The mouse trap was a five-gallon plastic bucket filled with two inches of water. You put peanut butter just below the bucket's rim, and the mice would fall into the bucket when reaching for the peanut butter and then drown in the water. They were effective traps but not effective enough to stop the infestation of mice.

Wednesday started with an immediate 1,300-foot climb to the White Cap Mountain summit. On the way up the mountain, we saw moose droppings and moose tracks at several locations. None of us had seen a moose in the wild before, which became a preoccupation for the rest of the hike. The climb to the summit was mostly from rock-to-rock steps that the trail maintainers placed to create a rock staircase. The summit was at 3,644 feet and a unique experience for all of us. The wind picked up significantly so that if you held out a handkerchief, it would blow perfectly horizontally. There was a frost covering on the trees, and it was cold enough that we pulled out our thermal coats. It was the first time I had experienced the dramatic changes that can occur when hiking in higher elevations. It was an exhilarating experience and one of the trip's highlights. We then hiked Hay Mountain, West Point, and Gulf Hagas Mountain.

We encountered two different aspects of hiking on this trip that we never experienced in Pennsylvania. The first was the quantity and size of the roots going across the trail. The roots, coupled with the steepness of the climb, created numerous and frequent natural steps of 18-plus inches. We called these "gut-busters," and they gave us a real workout. The second was caused by the depth and height of the mountains. In Pennsylvania, you see the summit, hike the mountain, then reach the summit, and it is over. In Maine, you see what you think is the summit, but it turns out to be a hill on the top that must be climbed on the way to the summit. We began to call these "false summits." We had to adjust our brains not to get too excited as we approached the top because there was likely another hill or two to climb before we reached the actual summit.

At about this point in the hike, a group of college-aged thru-hikers frolicked past us on the trail. They were energetic and euphoric as they pushed on towards their final destination. We were middle-aged, desk-softened weekend hikers; they were youthful, trail-hardened thru-hikers. They commented that the trail through this section was much easier than expected, and we were becoming increasingly demoralized as they quickly skipped out of sight.

Our morale was low at this point. There was some murmuring as we questioned the distance of the hike we chose, the number of climbs and descents we included each day, and whether all of this suffering was worth the 12-hour drive north. Most things worth doing have their costs. The value in doing difficult things in life is the endurance and character that it develops in you. After reading many accounts written by various thru-hikers, I found that each had many low points throughout their six-month journeys. The fact that only one in four completes their journey proves the physical and emotional pains that a thru-hiker must endure.

In Romans 5:3-4 (NLT), Paul writes, "We can rejoice, too, when we run into problems and trials, for we know that they help us develop endurance. And endurance develops strength of character, and character strengthens our confident hope of salvation". The idea of rejoicing when we encounter problems is sometimes challenging for me to accept. I don't doubt that the Apostle Paul did rejoice when he ran into problems. There are clear examples in the Scriptures, including an account when Paul was chained to a prison wall and was singing hymns while he hung there. Intellectually, I know that problems help develop endurance. Endurance develops strength of character. Character strengthens our hope of salvation. But when the problems hit, even though I realize that all this character development will happen, rejoicing is not my first response. However, as the years go by, and I see God's salvation repeatedly, it is easier to rejoice now than a few years ago.

As you read this scripture in Romans, you can see how character is built through a process: problems develop endurance, endurance develops character, and character strengthens our hope. Repeat. Repeat. Repeat. The more problems we experience, the more our hope is strengthened. It is not that we are instantly turned into people who rejoice when they run into problems, but it is a response that we develop as we continue to put our faith in God.

What is your response to problems? Are you developing into someone whose first response is to trust in God and rejoice when issues occur? Whether you are a thru-hiker or a weekend hiker, the challenges in life and on the trail help you develop endurance and character as you voyage on the path of life.

After Gulf Hagas Mountain, we descended 2,000 feet to the West Branch of the Pleasant River, where we set up camp a short distance from the water. It was a picturesque setting, and it was nice to escape the mouse population in the shelters. This was a 13-mile day with four significant climbs, and we were ready for a good night's rest. In the middle of the night, we woke up to the commotion of Butch moving the location of his tent. It turns out that Butch put his tent on top of a mouse nest, and they chewed a hole in his tent and then his food bag. As word spread in the mouse community, the mice began running over his head between his tent and his tent fly. So much for a peaceful night's sleep away from the shelter mice!

We rolled out of our tents Thursday morning and had breakfast, which included sharing a bagel with Butch, who lost one to the mice. We then made an immediate 1,000-foot climb. We climbed Chairback Mountain, Columbus Mountain, Third Mountain, and Fourth Mountain and began our ascent up Barren Mountain to reach our night destination, the Cloud Pond Shelter. We hiked 11 miles Thursday with over 2,000 feet of climbs. We began to settle into a routine of walking, eating, and sleeping. As I have mentioned, you experience a rhythm as you hike for a few days. The complexities of life are put on hold, and your priorities become walking, eating, and sleeping. While I am in awe of what the thru-hikers can accomplish, I sense the rhythm they must slip into on their much longer journey.

We settled in the shelter and took a refreshing dip in Cloud Pond. Although the average temperatures in Maine for early

October range from 35 to 60 degrees, we were experiencing record-breaking temperatures into the upper 70s. While this made it possible for us to enjoy a dip, it was still a rather bone-chilling one that was only long enough to rinse off the sweat and then quickly head back to the shoreline. The high temperatures also added to the challenge of our elevation climbs during each day's hike. Our preference would have been for the temperatures to be on the cooler side, but we were thankful that we experienced no rainfall during the entire hike.

On Friday morning, we completed the climb up Barren Mountain and explored the fire tower at the summit. Knowing it would be a shorter day with only nine miles of hiking, we took an extended break at this summit and even napped for a little while. We descended off of Barren Mountain and started to follow Long Pond Stream. The temperature rose to 79 degrees; we had time on our side and couldn't resist taking a dip at the base of Slugundy Falls.

Our original plan was to camp for the night at Wilson Valley Shelter, but it was full of other hikers, so we hiked on, looking for a better location. We set up camp about a mile down the trail at Big Wilson Stream. This was to be our final night on the trail. It was a scenic setting on a large stream with an ideal campsite. Our morale was high, and we finished our ongoing game of rummy, which we had started on Tuesday night. The final score was Dave at 1085, Dwayne at 1295, with Butch winning at 1340. Butch took a picture of the score sheet for future bragging rights.

Saturday would be a ten-mile hike to Jack's truck. The whole day was at lower elevations, and we passed a lot of water, including Little Wilson Stream, Mud Pond, North Pond, Leeman Brook, Lily Pond, Bell Pond, and Spectacle Pond. We spent a fair amount of time exploring and taking photos at

Little Wilson Falls, which, at 57 feet, is the highest waterfall on the AT and one of the highest in Maine.[15]

We arrived at Jack's truck and began the trip back to Pennsylvania. In case you were wondering, we never saw a moose in the wild. Jack made a case that we should go to the local petting zoo so we could at least claim to have seen a moose, but he was outvoted, and we began the "race" home.

---

[15]Ray Ronan, *The Appalachian Trail Guide to Maine* (Augusta, MA: Maine Appalachian Trail Club, 2004), 75.

Chapter Eight

TRAIL FOOD

Our debate continued, with Butch advocating for Red Velvet Cheesecake and me promoting the superiority of White Chocolate Macadamia Nut Caramel Drizzle Cheesecake. They were both dessert selections on the Cheesecake Factory's menu, and we were each entitled to our opinions as to which was the best, but it showed what your mindset becomes after you are on the trail for a few days.

Butch and I were two days into a three-day hike on the Chuck Keiper Trail in the Sproul State Forest in Pennsylvania. The Chuck Keiper Trail is a 50-mile loop cut in half by a three-mile connector trail, allowing hikers to choose between a 33-mile western loop or a 22-mile eastern loop.[16] The loops are

---

[16]Jeff Mitchell, *Backpacking Pennsylvania* (Mechanicsburg, PA: Stackpole Books, 2005), 187.

in a remote area and are very lightly used. This results in the trail being a little overgrown at times, but it also allows you to see more wildlife than you will on other, more popular trails. There is a significant black bear population, and I spotted wild brook trout in several streams. This is a more challenging hike, with much of the trail being on the sides of the mountain. You are often walking on the side of the hill, making it hard to get your footing, especially when leaves are on the trail.

We would be hiking the 33-mile western loop. We started on a Friday in August with a 13-mile hike planned to our first night's campsite along Yost Run. The trail was marked with orange blazes, and the section that previously followed Yost Run was rerouted to avoid high water flows. Since it was summer and there was low water flow, we decided to follow the old route, now marked with blue blazes. This decision was a big mistake. The blue blazes were not well maintained and were very hard to follow. In addition, the trail was overgrown with stinging nettles. These plants have skin-piercing hair follicles that release chemicals into your skin, causing inflammation. We put on our rain gear for added protection, but we moved at a snail's pace between the poorly marked trail and the overgrown nettles. We arrived at our site as the sun was retreating after a long day on the trail. We set up our camp and began to prepare our dinner.

Days like this make it clear why your backpacking meals should be easy to prepare, clean up, and be high in calories to replenish lost energy. My evening bite typically consists of a dehydrated packaged meal. You open the package, add boiling water, and let it sit to hydrate. You then eat the meal from the package and pack it for disposal later. As you can see, it is quick and easy, and there are no dishes to clean after you eat. Various manufacturers make dehydrated meals, and some of my favorites are made by backpackers who have created

Trail Food

their own versions and are now marketing them. Try a variety of vendors so you don't get bored having the same meals repeatedly.

I hope my description of the evening meal doesn't make it sound too unappetizing. After all, who wants to eat out of a plastic bag? Sitting down for the evening meal with your buddies is one of the highlights of each day's hike. You spend the day walking, burning calories, and snacking on trail mix and energy bars. As you look at the map and realize you are on the last few miles for the day, you start looking forward to setting up camp and enjoying your evening meal.

Some backpackers put a lot of time and energy into preparing healthier, more elaborate meals on the trail. I don't fault those who prepare a stir-fried medley of fresh vegetables and rice, and I will gladly eat it if you have any leftovers! However, it is days like the one that Butch and I just had that make me glad when I can prepare and eat supper in 10 to 15 minutes. Most of that time is spent waiting for the meal to hydrate, and zero time is spent cleaning up. There is a well-known saying in backpacking circles that you are bound to hear sooner or later — "hike your own hike." The meaning is simple: when on the trail, do what works for you.

My first stove to boil the water was a white gas stove that was a little tricky to use and heavy because you also had to pack a white gas fuel canister. The fuel canister had to be pressurized with a pump, and sometimes, when I lit the stove, there was a flash of flames. I was getting the hang of the system when I stopped by our local outfitter to pick up some things for my next backpacking trip. While browsing the merchandise, the sales clerk behind the counter asked me, "Have you seen the new Jetboil® stove?" He then proceeded to give me a demonstration. He put a Jetboil® stove on the sales counter, attached the small isobutane fuel canister, added a cup of water, ignited the stove, and had boiling water for a cup of tea within two minutes. I knew then, even at the $105 price tag, that I had to have a Jetboil® stove. I purchased the stove and then contemplated how I would tell Cindy and where I would get the money to pay for it!

In addition to the dehydrated meal, I sometimes have instant pudding for dessert. I prepackage half a package of instant pudding mixed with powdered instant milk in a zip-lock bag. When I am ready to eat, I add a cup of cold water and shake. In a few minutes, I have instant pudding that I eat out of the zip-lock bag. The bag can then be packed out for disposal later. Again, the focus is on easy preparation, cleanup, and high-calorie content.

For breakfast, I prepackage instant oatmeal with nuts and raisins in a zip-lock bag. I add hot water and then eat out of the bag, which, again, can be packed out for disposal later. I also have a bagel with peanut butter and a cup of coffee. I pack an assortment of energy bars, trail mix, and nuts for lunch. I snack on these items throughout the day each time we stop for a break.

Regardless of what you eat on the trail, the most important thing is drinking plenty of water. You should drink water frequently, whether you feel like it or not, to ensure you stay hydrated. My preferred water purification method is a ultraviolet light water purifier, which purifies the water through ultraviolet light. The ultraviolet light water purifier drains regular batteries in less than one outing, but lithium batteries last several trips. I carry backup batteries, which I have had to use on more than one trip, and I also carry iodine tablets as a backup system.

It is also good to have other backpackers in your group carry their own purification systems so that you can help each other out if needed. Some downsides of the ultraviolet light water purifier are that the ultraviolet light could break if dropped, and

Trail Food

it doesn't remove small particles floating in the water. A more reliable system is the traditional pump filter, but it takes much longer to fill a liter bottle with a pump filter than with a ultraviolet light water purifier. I once ran into a married couple on the Black Forest Trail who only had a ultraviolet light water purifier, but its batteries had died. I spent the next 15 minutes purifying water for them to use for the remainder of their trip.

I have limited how much water I carry on different occasions and regretted it. You are at the base of a mountain next to a free-flowing stream and are trying to decide if you want to fill your water bottles full or just half full, knowing you have a 1,000-foot mountain to climb. You look at the map and see a blue line that indicates another stream halfway down the other side that intersects the trail ahead of you. You decide only to fill your liter bottles halfway and reduce the weight to carry up the mountain by two pounds. As you climb, you ration how much water you drink, just in case that blue line is only a seasonal stream. You make it over the mountain to where the stream is supposed to be, and you find a dry creek bed. You gambled and lost, and now you must continue rationing your water until the next stream. Your mouth and lips are starting to feel dry, and you are feeling a little lightheaded and tired. You begin to worry that the next stream may also be dry, and you are now feeling panicked and slightly dehydrated. A desperate feeling comes from being thirsty and not being sure of when or where you will get your next drink.

> *In the same way that we physically thirst for water, we can spiritually thirst for a relationship with God, as conveyed in Psalms 42:1 (NLT); "As the deer longs for streams of water, so I long for you, O God. I thirst for God, the living God."*

The deer pants for water because it needs water to survive. It is not a matter of refreshment for the deer; it is a matter of life and death. In the same sense, our longing for God is a matter of spiritual life or death and eternal life or death. Furthermore, the deer's desire for water (and ours) is instinctual. It is a natural and inborn desire. We do not develop the longing for water like coffee or other beverages. Physically, we instinctually long for the water our bodies need to survive. Spiritually, we instinctually long for an eternal relationship with God.

To those who do not have a relationship with God, I encourage you to yield to the longing in your heart and invite God into your life. God placed that longing inside you and is waiting for you to respond.

To the person who has already established a relationship with God, I caution you not to let it grow stale. Doing a periodic and honest assessment of your relationship with God is valuable. Do you still thirst for God as you did when you were new in your faith? If not, let God know that you want to renew your relationship with him and be intentional about reading the Bible and praying daily. God will refresh and renew you as you seek him.

Something I have found over the years to help me refocus on God is to have a two or three-day fast, where I drink water but eat no food. When it is my usual time to eat during a fast, I pray and read the Bible. This discipline is also valuable when you have an essential decision to make or want God's direction as you set goals for yourself in the new year. Consider consulting with your physician before you do a fast if you have some physical challenge that fasting may aggravate. When I fast in this manner, I say to God that I desire him more than the food I thoroughly enjoy. This sacrifice is an amazing way to connect with God while on the path of life.

Drinking, carrying, and replenishing your water supply should be a preoccupation when backpacking. You don't want to risk dehydration on the trail, and water is essential to our bodies' proper functioning.

Butch and I had a quick breakfast, packed up camp, committed our day's hike to God, and hit the trail. Soon after we left our campsite, we came to a 15-foot waterfall on Yost Run. Later that day, we were on a raised railroad bed and saw significant bear scat on the trail. Before too long, we spooked a large black bear off of the trail. It ran down the hill next to the railroad grade, up the side of the mountain, and out of sight. The speed and agility that the large bear had was impressive, and it kept us on our toes for the rest of the hike. We were now following Eddy Lick Run and came upon a deserted splash dam. This was one of the areas where I saw some wild trout.

As an avid fly fisherman, I am always looking for a wild trout population. I make a mental note, but these areas are generally too far from my home for fishing trips. I took my fly rod backpacking several times but was too tired in the evening to do anything more than eat and sleep. It never made sense for me to mix my fly fishing and backpacking passions. I have thought about a trip where I backpack into an area and set up a base camp to fish from, but that has yet to materialize. This location is an area to consider doing that.

After another 13-mile day of hiking, we chose a campsite along Swamp Branch Creek and began our routine of gathering firewood, making a fire, eating dinner, playing rummy, and getting a good ten-plus hours of sleep. Sunday was an uneventful hike back to the car for our ride home.

As I always do, I unpacked as soon as I got home. I hang my tent and sleeping bag to let them dry out before storing them, and then clean and store the rest of my equipment, like my stove, ultraviolet light water purifier, trekking poles, and backpack. I showered, and Cindy waited for me with a cup of coffee. I then downloaded my hike photos onto a computer so I could show Cindy what the hike was like. I was enjoying my cup of coffee and describing the pictures to Cindy when we got to one that I took of one of my meals. She saw the Jetboil® stove I had purchased but never told her about it, so she asked, "What's that?" Oh well! I was snagged and had to explain why this stove was so much better than my original stove!

Butch and I continued our debate about Red Velvet Cheesecake and White Chocolate Macadamia Nut Caramel Drizzle Cheesecake for several years to come. Whenever we ate at the Cheesecake Factory, we would send each other photos to continue the debate. The last time I was at the Cheesecake Factory and ordered a White Chocolate Macadamia Nut Caramel Drizzle Cheesecake, I was told it was discontinued. Huh, I guess Butch was right after all.

Chapter Nine

SHARING THE PASSION

As my three daughters started to date and then married, it was nice having some guys around to talk sports, fishing, and the outdoors. I shared my passion for backpacking with my sons-in-law and one by one, they each accepted invitations to go backpacking with me. We naturally want to share our passions with others, especially those we care about or are interested in getting to know better. This was certainly the case with my sons-in-law, so it became my priority to allow each to experience backpacking.

Surprisingly, the first one to go backpacking with me was my youngest son-in-law, Steve, and he was only dating my daughter Kendra at the time. It showed me what a brave young man he was to venture into the woods for a weekend with the father of the girl he had a thing for. I planned a two-day and one-night backpacking trip on the Black Forest Trail in Pennsylvania's Little Grand Canyon. My hiking buddy Butch and I had hiked most of the Black Forest Trail the previous autumn but had to cut our hike short when we spent a day on a cabin porch to stay out of the rain. This hike was an opportunity for me to finish the section of trail that Butch and I never completed and a chance to get to know Steve better.

One of the conversations I have with someone I am taking backpacking for the first time is to describe what they should wear on their feet. Sometimes, they will have work boots that will suffice. If they need to purchase something new, I will encourage them to get boots that are lighter weight and offer good support at the same time. I stay away from suggesting waterproof options that will be more costly. This may be their first and last backpacking trip, and I want to help them keep their costs down. I also let them know the importance of breaking the boot in before they hit the trail. Once Steve had the boots he would use, I spent an evening with Steve, giving him the backpacking equipment I was lending him and explaining what kind of clothes and food to pack. Lastly, I showed him how to load his backpack. It can be a lot of information for someone to absorb, so I have a printout I give newbies to refer to as they prepare for the trip. I want to provide first-timers with as much information as possible to prepare them. I am glad Jack did that as I prepared for my first hike. (See Appendix 1 for the handout I give to newbies) (Appendix 1 can also be downloaded at www.backpackingandthepathoflife.com)

The day came, and Steve and I made the three-hour drive north. I would have been a nervous wreck if I were Steve—spending a weekend with the father of the girl that I had my eye on! We parked my SUV in the gravel parking lot at the end of Naval Run Road and mounted our backpacks. I prayed, asking for God's protection, and then we followed a mountain

Sharing the Passion

road to Naval Run. Just ten minutes into our hike, Steve miss-stepped crossing Naval Run and ended up with a boot full of water. I had Steve change his socks and explained how important it is to hike with dry socks to avoid blisters.

We followed an unmarked path paralleling Naval Run to where it intersects with the Black Forest Trail. After a half-mile or so, I asked Steve, "How does the backpack feel? How are your feet?" It is better to make early adjustments than have a newbie develop a blister or sore and ruin the rest of their backpacking experience. Steve said that he felt good, and we continued to hike on.

The Black Forest Trail began making a 700-foot climb as soon as we started hiking it. When we got to the summit, I could see a look of concern on Steve's face, as if hiking the mountain was more challenging than he had expected. I have seen that look before, and it is the initial shock of how difficult it is to walk uphill with 30 pounds on your back. I knew he would be fine, and we continued to move forward, enjoying several vistas on the ridge over the next few miles.

We came to an old, weathered sign that read, "800 Feet to Large Virgin Hemlock," and followed the short trail to see the 43-inch round old-growth hemlock. The trail guide explained that the tree was on the border between two properties, and neither property owner claimed the tree, so it was never cut down.[17] It was an impressive tree and a hint of what the forest used to look like before woodcutters harvested its lumber.

I have had several post-hike meals at The Hotel Manor, which sits near Pine Creek, where we were hiking. The restaurant has black and white photos from the early 1900s that

---

[17]Pennsylvania Department of Conservation and Natural Resources, *Black Forest Trail* (South Williamsport, PA: Tiadaghton Forest Fire Fighter's Association, 2003), 22.

showed what the harvested mountains looked like. They were stripped down to mounds of dirt, rocks, and mud. It is heartbreaking to see the devastation caused by logging this beautiful forest. You could argue that the forest did grow back, but the truth is that the erosion caused by the logging methods made it impossible for the forest to ever return to what it once was. It is mind-boggling to consider that this practice occurred throughout the state and that very few virgin trees remain.

After several moderate climbs and descents, it started to rain, and we put our rain gear on. We made one last 400-foot rocky climb to Foster Hollow Pond, where we would be camping for the night. The steep rocky climb was a little tricky in the rain, and Steve was relieved once we arrived at our campsite. It was an eight-mile day with a fair amount of elevation changes. The elevation changes made it a challenging day so that Steve could feel like he had accomplished something, but not so hard that Steve would get the idea that I was trying to punish him for showing interest in my daughter. There was a cabin with a porch next to the pond, so we took refuge under the porch roof as we prepared and ate supper. The rain let up, and we set up our tents. The ground was pretty soggy, so instead of making the customary fire, we headed to our tents for the night.

We had breakfast under the cabin porch and then hiked three additional miles on the Black Forest Trail that morning. When hiked clockwise, these three miles were the last of the 42-mile Black Forest Trail. The hiker experiences a beautiful vista before descending back to Slate Run, where the trail begins. It is a rather dramatic finish to the hike, with the trail following the ridge to a point where it suddenly drops off out of sight. You are left standing there at the end of the ridge, looking down at what looks like an impossible climb down. Multiple switchbacks help you get off the mountain, and you are thankful that you are hiking down this section of trail, not up the steep grade. Once we were back to Slate Run, we had a one-mile road walk back to my SUV parked at Naval Run. I was glad that Steve and I had the chance to do this hike together. It helped me get to know Steve better and gave him a glimpse into how passionate I was about the outdoors and backpacking.

When you enjoy something and are passionate about it, it is only natural that you want to share it with others so they can experience it. Thankfully, that is what Jack did when he took me on my first backpack trip. I am doing the same when I take my family, friends, and co-workers backpacking as well.

When it comes to sharing your passion for Jesus with others, it is much more than sharing an enjoyable hobby or pastime; it may be the difference between eternal life or eternal separation from God. The final instructions Jesus gave his followers may be the most essential instructions he gave them as well. In Matthew 28:19-20 (NLT), he commands "... go and make disciples of all the nations, baptizing them in the name of the Father and the Son and the Holy Spirit. Teach these new disciples to obey all the commands I have given you." The instructions are clear: we have been given to share with others so that they can be Christ followers, too.

Telling others about your relationship with Jesus can be intimidating. You don't want to offend them by being judgmental about how they live their lives. That is between them and God; not for you to get in the middle of. You also want to avoid coming off as a spiritual know-it-all by presenting yourself as someone who has all the answers. I know for myself that there are some spiritual things that I question, and that will have to wait until I get to heaven for me to understand more clearly.

You should share from your heart what having a personal relationship with Jesus means to you. I love how Peter talks about what this exchange should look like in 1 Peter 3:15-16 (NLT); "... if someone asks about your hope as a believer, always be ready to explain it. But do this in a gentle and respectful way..."

Barry was the owner of the construction company I worked for and my direct boss. It took a few years for Barry to gain confidence in my abilities and to trust my judgment. There were several situations where we had to make critical business decisions. As I offered my perspective and the situations were resolved, Barry would say to me, "You look at things so differently; where did you come up with that idea?" I told Barry several times that it was not my idea and then went on to explain. "When I have a challenge or important decision, I pray and ask God for wisdom. The answer is not usually immediate but comes to me when I need it. The Holy Spirit living within me is my guide who gives me these ideas."

As time passed, Barry retired and rarely came into the office. Regardless, I would keep him in the loop on essential matters and update him on how things were going. I had some paperwork for him to sign, and I usually would have had one of his sons deliver to him. This time, however, Barry was experiencing some health challenges, and I felt compelled to personally go to his home to have him sign the documents. As I arrived, Barry sat on a stone wall in front of his house. I sat beside him, and we talked about business, politics, the outdoors, and other common interests. I asked Barry if I could ask him a spiritual question, and he said, "Sure." I explained that this was a diagnostic question to help me understand where he was spiritually.[18]

"Barry, if you died and were standing at heaven's gates and asked why you should be let into heaven, what would you say?" Barry responded, "I would say that I believe in God. Then I would tell him I am worried about who will care for my wife once I am gone." Then he hesitated and said, "I know God will care for her."

I responded, "Good answers, Barry. Some might say that they should be let into heaven because they are a good person or that they should be let into heaven because they go to church. The Bible tells us that our entrance into heaven is based on our belief and faith in God. It is not based on our works but a gift." I asked Barry if he prayed to ask God for this gift. He said, "No," so I asked him if I could lead him in a prayer to help him do that. He said, "Yes," so I led him in a prayer where he confessed his sins and asked Jesus for the gift of eternal life.

It was a privilege to help Barry solidify his relationship with God. He now knew for sure where he stood with God. The dialogue was not awkward or unnatural—it was a conversation between two friends with mutual

---

[18]D. James Kennedy, *Evangelism Explosion 4th Edition* (Carol Stream, Illinois: Tyndale House Publishers, 1996), 77.

respect. This conversation was in June; Barry went on to be with the Lord in October.

As you travel on the path of life, make sure you share with others your hope in God.

Steve and I began the ride home, and we now had this new shared experience to talk about. I could tell Steve was exhausted from the hike and struggling to keep his eyes open. I suggested he nap for a little while I drove home, which he did. This hike didn't scare off Steve too badly because he married my daughter Kendra three years later, and he did a second hike with me five years after that.

Chapter Ten
THE FULL BACKPACK

As my backpacking equipment inventory grew, it allowed me to take family, friends, and co-workers hiking with me. I planned one such hike with my son-in-law Brett and my hiking buddy Butch. Butch was Brett's youth pastor before Brett and my daughter Ashley got married. Butch and I hiked several times together in the past, and including Brett in one of our hikes seemed like a great idea! I prefer to hike in an area I am familiar with when I take someone hiking for the first time because I know the trail conditions and what to expect. As I considered the individuals who would be hiking, it seemed like a return trip to Dolly Sods Wilderness Area would be perfect!

This trip to Dolly Sods was eight years after my first backpacking experience and my first time back to that area since that hike. It was sentimental for me to return to the place where it all began and to be able to share that experience with Brett and Butch.

I had the standard conversation with Brett about the importance of a good pair of hiking boots, and it turned out that he already had a pair that he wore when he did yard work. I also described the clothing and food he should pack for the trip. Lastly, I spent an evening with Brett to give him the backpacking equipment I was lending him and to show him how to load the backpack.

There are some general guidelines about loading a backpack, but many things come down to personal preferences developed over time. I show newbies how I pack my bag and let them figure out what works best for them. After all, you must hike your own hike. I load my backpack with a priority on convenience and weight distribution. The items I will use during the day are packed near the top of the pack. When I get to camp, I want to unload logically as I set up camp. Also, I like the weight distributed evenly so that the backpack is not lop-sided.

The first item I put in the backpack is my sleeping bag, lying on its side. The sleeping bag is the bulkiest item you will load, and this expands your pack so that it is ready to receive the rest of your equipment. Also, the sleeping bag will be the last item you take out of your backpack when you set up camp, and this will keep it protected until your tent is set up.

I put the tent in its bag, with the fly in the bottom, then the stakes, and the shell on top. I don't fold and roll the fly and shell in the manner it came from the manufacturer because it will get a memory of where the folds are. Instead, I stuff it in its bag, which is also a lot quicker and easier than folding it. I then put the tent bag on its side, on top of the sleeping bag. If the tent is wet when I pack up camp, I put it in a plastic bag to keep it from leaking water onto my sleeping bag.

The Full Backpack

I put everything I will need for meals in a waterproof sack. This includes a spoon, coffee cup, and food supplies. The sack is waterproof because you will hang it over a tree limb to protect it from wildlife. The food sack is laid on its side, on top of the tent bag.

The last main bag I put in the backpack, on top of the food sack, is the clothes sack. This holds my extra clothes and is on the top if I need something during the day. Starting in the bottom of the sack and working to the top are two small plastic bags I carry to wear over my socks if my boots get wet, a small plastic bag to hold dirty laundry, a few hankies, socks for each day, underwear for each day, knit hat, and a long sleeve T-shirt. I wear the same dirty outer clothes to hike each day. I wear the additional long-sleeved T-shirt and rain suit in the evening at camp. My rain suit is the last item in the clothes sack, so it is easy to access in the event of rain.

I now load smaller items in front of the bulkier items I described. I push the air mattress to the bottom of the backpack so that it can be unloaded at the same time as the sleeping bag.

I put my stove on top of the air mattress. It is designed to hold its own fuel canister and has a stand that helps it sit on uneven ground.

On top of the stove, I place a one-gallon zip-lock bag that holds miscellaneous equipment. This bag contains a clothesline rope, rope to hang the food sack, a fire starter, matches, a headlamp, and extra batteries. Using a zip-lock bag is handy because I can see what items are in it at a glance.

In addition to the miscellaneous equipment bag, I have a one-gallon zip-lock bag to hold my toiletries, which include toothpaste, toothbrush, biodegradable liquid soap, toilet paper, and handy wipes.

The last item in the main body of my backpack is a one-gallon zip lock bag to hold my medical items, which includes aspirin, moleskin, first-aid cream, a nail care kit, matches, and iodine tablets as a backup for water purification.

The top lid of the backpack contains the following:

- The food I will be eating during that day's hike
- Ultraviolet light water purifier for water purification
- Backpack cover
- A large plastic trash bag

Most backpacks are not waterproof, so you need to cover yours with a backpack cover if it starts to rain. The large plastic trash bag is used to hold my tent if it is wet when I put it in my backpack so that it doesn't get other items wet. I also use the large plastic trash bag when I first get to camp if it rains. I first pull out the large plastic trash bag, then use it to hold all the contents of the backpack to protect them from the rain until the tent is set up.

On the outside of the backpack, I hang a sitting pad wrapped around tent poles, water bottles, gloves, and sandals. The gloves are used when it is cold out and when I collect firewood as we set up camp. The sandals are readily available in case we have to cross a stream, but I also wear the sandals over socks in the evening as my camp shoes.

The last item I put on my backpack is my fleece jacket, which I place under the top lid. Many backpackers use a fleece jacket as a mid-weight layer, an essential piece of backpacking clothing. Let's say it is early November, and you are ready to start hiking in the morning. There is a chill in the air, so you wear your gloves and mid-weight layer. You start hiking up a hill, which is common after you camp for the night in a ravine next to a stream, and you begin to warm up. Before you break a sweat, you remove your mid-weight layer and possibly your gloves for the rest of your morning hike.

The Full Backpack

You are now hiking in your breathable long-sleeve T-shirt, and it is surprising how it is enough to keep you warm, even during many winter days. It might only be 30 degrees out, but the heat your hiking generates is enough to keep you comfortable. You may even break a sweat, quickly evaporating through your breathable T-shirt. You are now ready to stop for a break. You remove your backpack and put on your mid-weight layer to avoid getting a chill. When your break is over, and you are ready to start hiking again, remove the mid-weight layer and remount your backpack.

Throughout the day, and even once you are in camp for the evening, you are monitoring how your body responds to the conditions and responding accordingly. While hiking, you want to stay hydrated and, at the same time, not let your body's sweat be trapped in your clothing. When you are in camp for the evening, you want to let your sweaty clothes hang out to dry and wear your dry camp clothes. This is another time that the mid-weight layer is used so that you do not get chilled while in camp in the evening. (See Appendix 2 for my detailed packing list and Appendix 3 for illustrations of how I load my backpack) (Appendix 2 can also be downloaded at www.backpacking andthepathoflife.com)

Part of the allure of backpacking is that you have everything you need on your back to survive for a few days in the woods. It gives you a great sense of freedom and independence! Carrying all this on your back makes for a full backpack, and I always caution newbies to consider everything they put in their pack carefully. It might be nice to have specific items once they set up camp, but the downside is that every item adds weight, and they must carry that weight on their back.

As you experience backpacking, you will be surprised at how little you need daily to survive. You don't want to carry unnecessary items that add weight. The other extreme would be to forego essential items, which, if eliminated, could put you at risk for sickness or harm. There is a balance between carrying too much weight and not carrying the essentials you need for a safe hike.

The essentials you need to carry on your back are water, protection from the elements, and food. Having a way to carry and purify water is the highest priority. Protection from the elements includes your rain gear and shelter. Certain clothing can indeed protect you from the elements, but this is an area where many people overpack. Eliminate redundant clothing articles and accept that you will smell bad after spending a few days in the woods. The last essential is food, and you should focus on food that is high in calories to replenish what you burn each day while hiking. I often pack more food than I need and have food left over when I am finished hiking. I need to start packing less food.

Just like you must pack the essentials on your hiking trip to sustain you, there are essentials that will sustain you spiritually. Ephesians 6:11-17 (NLV) describes these: "Put on all of God's armor so that you will be able to stand firm against all strategies of the Devil. For we are not fighting against flesh-and-blood enemies, but against evil rulers and authorities of the unseen world, against mighty powers in this dark world, and against evil spirits in the heavenly places. Therefore, put on every piece of God's armor so you will be able to resist the enemy in the time of evil. Then after the battle you will still be standing firm. Stand your ground, putting on the belt of truth and the body armor of God's righteousness. For shoes, put on the peace that comes from the Good News so that you will be fully prepared. In addition to all of these, hold up the shield of faith to stop the fiery arrows

The Full Backpack

of the Devil. Put on salvation as your helmet, and take the sword of the Spirit, which is the word of God."

This scripture has a lot to unpack, but it is worth the effort. It describes our spiritual journey as a battle against the Devil. We are told that we must put on every piece of God's armor to win the fight.

We are to wear the belt of truth. The Devil, also known as "the deceiver," is trying to confuse us and distort the truth. As believers, our sins are forgiven, and we have been adopted into God's family. In our spiritual journey, we should wear the belt of truth and not be deceived by the Devil's lies.

We are to wear the body armor of God's righteousness. As believers, we are seen as righteous by God. This is not because of our actions or goodness but because of what Jesus did for us on the cross. In our spiritual journey, we can confidently know that we are righteous or in right standing with God because our sins are forgiven.

We are to wear the shoes of peace from the Good News. The Good News is that Jesus died for our sins and rose from the dead. As believers, we are to take this Good News to others.

We are to hold up the shield of faith to protect us from the Devil's fiery arrows. Our faith that God exists is what defines us as believers. The Devil will try to attack us, but our faith in God is our shield.

We are to wear the helmet of salvation. The helmet of salvation protects our head, where our beliefs and thoughts are formed. As believers, we must guard our thoughts and not allow the Devil to influence us.

Lastly, we are to carry the sword of the Spirit, the word of God, which is the Bible and guides us throughout our spiritual journey.

This whole section of scripture uses symbolic language to describe the armor we are to wear in our spiritual journey. Remember that, as a believer, you are in a real spiritual battle against the Devil, who is a real enemy. Humans are both physical and spiritual beings and we fight battles in both dominions. John Eldredge compares our situation to frogs who need an environment of both land and water to survive, they are amphibious. In a similar way, humans are amphibious in that they are living in both a physical and spiritual world. The physical is all around us and hard to ignore, but don't underestimate the importance of fighting the daily spiritual battle through prayer and reading the Bible. This is where the physical and spiritual battels are fought and won.

Just as water, shelter, and food are essential to your physical needs, the armor is essential to your spiritual needs. You need to carry the full armor with you on the path of life and on your hiking trip. The best thing is that the armor is one essential that adds zero weight to your backpack!

Brett, Butch and I parked at the Blackbird Knob Trailhead and, after studying the map for a few minutes, decided to hike to Lions Head, where we would spend our first night on the trail. The high point of any trip to Dolly Sods is spending a night at the rock outcropping called Lions Head. We missed the access path when I was there the first time, so I kept my eyes focused on the trail this time. The access path looks more like a wildlife trail than a hiking trail and only had a small rock cairn to mark it. I can see why we missed the path when I was there eight years earlier. We spent the evening exploring Lions Head and camped under the summit's pine trees.

Other than a visit to Lions Head, every trip to Dolly Sods is unique. There are many interconnecting trails, and you inevitably take a different route each time you backpack there. In a typical hike, I lay out a hiking route ahead of time, but at Dolly Sods, you gather around the map as a group, someone suggests a trail or some combination of trails, and then the group decides what trails are going to be hiked for the day. The plan is created on the fly and makes for a different backpacking experience.

It is hard to imagine having anything but an enjoyable hike in Dolly Sods, and I am sure that Brett would agree. Brett is in good physical shape and enjoys the challenges of backpacking. He has the same planning gene as I do. I can picture him planning some hikes of his own in the future. I know that Dolly Sods birthed in me a desire to backpack more, and I hope that it did the same for Brett as well.

Chapter Eleven
HIKING WITH YOUR EYES OPEN

Uriah is married to my oldest daughter, Allie. Uriah's passion is hunting large game, and he has a friend with a hunting camp not far from the elk herd in northern Pennsylvania. Before colonization, elk roamed throughout the state of Pennsylvania, but by the 1860s, they remained only in Elk & Cameron counties. By the 1870s, no elk remained in Pennsylvania.[19] Several attempts were made to reintroduce Yellowstone Elk into Pennsylvania and in the 1990s the herd began to grow to its 2020 level of about 1,400.[20]

---

[19] Joe Kosack. "History of Pennsylvania Elk." www.pgc.pa.gov/Wildlife/WildlifeSpecies/Elk/Pages/HistoryofElkinPA.aspx (February 27, 2023).
[20] Jason Nark. "Elk, Pa.'s largest wild animal, have become a tourism boom in the northwest part of the state." www.inquirer.com/news/pennsylvania/elk-county-benezette-tourism-hunt-20210305.html (February 27, 2023).

Backpacking & the Path of Life

Uriah's friend holds an annual event near Elk County called "Shed Camp," when they hunt for antlers shed by elk. Uriah told me they would walk on the Quehanna Trail when hunting for dropped antlers and how remote and beautiful the area was. I researched the Quehanna Trail and later purchased a trail guide and maps for the area, hoping that I would have the chance to experience it as well.

The Quehanna Trail is a 73-mile loop with a connector trail and many other side trails enabling you to access the loop in various ways.[21] It took little convincing for me to talk Uriah into doing a hike on the Quehanna Trail since it was an area that he was interested in exploring because of its hunting opportunities. I planned a three-day, 22-mile trip in late May, where we would backpack the northern side of the oval loop. We drove to the Quehanna area on a Saturday morning in two vehicles, parking one where the Quehanna trail crosses the Quehanna Highway a few miles south of Medix Run. We drove to our starting point in the other vehicle where the trail crosses Wykoff Run Road.

We began hiking west on the Quehanna Trail as it followed the Laurel Draft. Many of the streams in this area are called "drafts." I did some research on why the streams were called "drafts," and I could find no conclusive explanation. What is interesting is how local history and culture can shape the area you are backpacking in, as reflected in the names of the trails, streams, ravines, hollows, mountains, knolls, knobs, and other land features.

These areas, untouched by development, offer a unique glimpse into the past. As you backpack through, you'll be transported to a different time, a snapshot of life as it was. An

---

[21] Ralph Seeley, *Foot Trails of the Moshannon State Forest*, (St. Mary's, PA: Quehanna Area Trails Club, 2001), 1.

excellent example is "Wild Cat Rocks," located on the southern leg of the Quehanna Trail, where I hiked with Uriah on a subsequent hike. There is a plaque in the Wild Cat Rocks area that explains that three wildcats were shot there in the 1940s. Historical events occur and areas are named for those events. Many years later, as you are backpacking through those areas, their names hint at the area's history. Pay attention to the names of the land features where you hike, and consider the history that led to those names.

We followed the magnificent Laurel Draft for a few miles and gradually climbed from 1,100 feet to 2,100 feet until we reached the summit. We were then treated to the Little Fork Vista, which gives you a view of rolling mountain after rolling mountain and a perspective of how remote and uninhabited this area is.

Not long after the vista, we came to the most impressive grove of white birch trees I have ever seen. It was a beautiful display, and Uriah commented on how much his son Judah would enjoy camping there. It would have been a nice spot to camp, but we still had a few more miles to hike until we reached our planned camping destination along Sanders Draft.

We soon reached Sanders Draft, and the trail crossed it several times as it cascaded down the mountainside. It was a narrow stream with a strong flow of transparent water that made its way through rhododendrons, lush ferns, and moss-covered rocks. We found an ideal campsite, and since this was Uriah's first time backpacking with me, I gave him a hand setting up his (my) tent, and then we gathered firewood. That day, we hiked seven miles, some of the most diverse and beautiful seven miles I have ever hiked in Pennsylvania. I could see why Uriah had an attraction to this wilderness area, and I was looking forward to our next day of hiking.

On Sunday morning, we followed Sanders Draft to where it flows into the much larger Red Run. The trail then followed

Red Run and then Porcupine Draft. Yes, this area has endless creeks, runs, and drafts, which all make for a beautiful hike. Porcupine Hollow was at 1,200 feet, and we climbed back to the summit at 2,200 feet. After a few miles on the summit, we were treated to another vista and reminder of what a remote wilderness this was.

We started dropping off the summit and realized we would soon be arriving where we had planned to camp for the night. Our original plan was to hike eight miles on this day and camp along Mix Run. As we dropped to about 1,800 feet, we came to an open grassy field that looked like an area elk might visit as dusk approached.

In the same area, we came to the headwaters of what would become Deible Run and wondered if this could be a spot where we could spend the night. There were some stagnant pools of water, which would not have been good to get water from, but as we followed the marshy ground, we reached a point where water springs percolated up out of the ground. We found a spot with flowing water deep enough to fill our water bottles, so we decided to spend the night by the spring and grassy area, hoping to be visited by some elk that evening. We weren't the first to ever camp here, which was evident by the fire ring and logs already assembled.

Headwaters have always intrigued me as a trout fisherman, and now that I was backpacking, I got to see how streams are formed. We were at 1,800 feet, close to the summit of the mountain, and water was coming up from the ground. As you follow a spring like this, it soon develops into a 12-inch-wide brook. A half-mile later, and after being joined by two additional brooks, it is now 24 inches wide and starting to take shape. After another half-mile and being joined by another 24-inch-wide stream, a viable stream flows throughout the summer and does not freeze solid during the winter. The stream may even support a population of wild brook trout. It

Hiking With Your Eyes Open

is impressive to see this occur as you follow the stream down the side of the mountain.

We never saw any elk Sunday evening, but it was worth changing our plans in case one of these massive animals wandered by our campsite. On Monday morning, we followed Deible Run to where it joined Mix Run and followed Mix Run. Lastly, we followed Silvermill Hollow Run a little before the trail took us back to our vehicle parked off Quehanna Highway. This was another seven-mile day of hiking through a beautiful wilderness area. Uriah and I went on to hike the southern leg of the Quehanna Trail two years later in the Fall. We didn't see any elk on that trip either, but we saw some hoof prints, droppings, and tree rubs that showed they were in the area.

I would not have noticed the signs of the elk if Uriah hadn't pointed them out to me. What you can miss on the trail is amazing if you aren't looking for it. As you hike, it is valuable to "hike with your eyes open" and take in all the sights, sounds, and smells to expand your hiking experience. I am not implying that you would ever hike with your eyes closed. I am talking about being intentional as you hike to look for the unusual, unexpected, and extraordinary.

When hiking with your eyes open, you genuinely appreciate the remoteness of the area as you gaze from a vista at the valley below. When hiking with your eyes open, you see the uniqueness of a meadow filled with white birch trees. When hiking with your eyes open, you consider why an area might be called Wild Cat Rocks and what it was like for the early settlers as they first explored the mountain you are now on. When hiking with your eyes open, you see firsthand how a high-altitude spring develops into a mountain stream.

Just as there is value in hiking with your eyes open, you should advance in your spiritual journey with your spiritual eyes open as well. When you walk with your spiritual eyes open and see your needs being taken care of, realize that it is God who is meeting the need. James 1:17 (NLT) reminds us, "Whatever is good and perfect is a gift coming down to us from God our Father, who created all the lights in the heavens."

When you walk with your spiritual eyes open and encounter others with needs, look on them with the same compassion that God does and consider 1 John 4:7-12 (NLT): "Dear friends, let us continue to love one another, for love comes from God. Anyone who loves is a child of God and knows God."

Our spiritual journey does not start each Sunday morning as we step into the church building and end when we head back home in our car. Our spiritual journey happens every minute of every day. 1 Thessalonians 5:16-18 (NLV) conveys what our spiritual journey should look like when it says, "Always be joyful. Never stop praying. Be thankful in all circumstances, for this is God's will for you who belong to Christ Jesus."

I challenge you to hike with your physical eyes open to get the most out of your backpacking experience. I challenge you to live with your spiritual eyes open as God guides you on the path of life.

I am so glad I got to experience this beautiful area that Uriah is so fond of. Hiking there is incredible, and getting to know Uriah better was great. I am so fortunate to have three fine sons-in-laws willing to go backpacking with me. It has been an excellent way to connect with each one of them, and I will always treasure the memories we created. They are all busy now with work and families, and scheduling trips is becoming harder and harder. When Uriah mentioned camping with Judah next to those white birch trees, it got me thinking: I need to order a few small backpacks for my grandkids to take them backpacking with me as they grow up. It's just another way to pass this passion on!

Chapter Twelve

THE REWARD

The agreement terms were set: if my daughter Ashley reached her goal weight, I would buy her a new bathing suit. If I reached my goal weight, Ashley would go backpacking with me. We both took the same approach to achieving our goals. We would reduce the quantities of food we ate, eliminate snacks, not eat anything after the evening meal, and exercise daily for 20 minutes. We were allowed two eating cheats each week and could skip one exercise session. Our regular updates via email helped us stay on track more than anything. We would share our victories, confess our cheats, and be each other's cheerleaders.

We reached our goals, and the day came for Ashley to pay up and join me on a hike. This new hiking partner was my reward for reaching my goal, but there was no resistance on

Ashley's part to be included in one of my backpacking trips. The hiking party involved Ashley, me, and Ashley's husband, Brett. I chose a 16-mile loop in northern Pennsylvania that joins the High Rock Trail, Loyalsock Trail, and the Loyalsock Link Trail to create a loop.[22] I had hiked the Loyalsock Trail a few years before with my hiking buddy Dave, but I had never hiked the loop before. The loop is a moderately difficult trail and an excellent hike for newbies. It was mid-April, and the plan was to hike six miles on Friday and camp at Tamarack Run, hike seven miles on Saturday and camp at Cold Run, and then hike three miles on Sunday back to my SUV.

The main benefit of a loop hike is that you only need one vehicle to get to the trailhead and back home. This saves on vehicle fuel and allows you to connect with the other hikers driving to and from the trailhead. It was nice spending time with Ashley and Brett, but it also gave me a chance to tell them what to expect on the hike. We parked my SUV at the World's End State Park and began our journey by taking the High Rock Trail to where it joins the Loyalsock Trail. Hikes often start with a climb, and this was no exception.

It was a moderate climb of 365 feet over a half-mile distance, but when it is your first time hiking up a hill carrying a backpack, the exertion it takes can come as a surprise. We reached the top, and Ashley said her socks were bunching up. I had her sit on a rock to remove her boots and fix her socks, and I could see the concern on her face. Without her saying a word, I could hear her say, "Dad, I didn't think it was going to be this difficult!" I reassured her this was the only climb for the day, the hardest for the hike, and that she was doing great!

---

[22]Jeff Mitchell, *Backpacking Pennsylvania* (Mechanicsburg, PA: Stackpole Books, 2005), 35.

The Reward

We continued hiking, but I didn't realize we had passed the Loyalsock Trail and kept walking on the High Rock Trail. We walked almost a half-mile downhill before I realized we weren't heading in the right direction. After staring at the map for a little, I decided we needed to turn around and retrace our steps back up the hill.

I had a map, as I always do, but I was not yet using GPS as a double check against what I was seeing on the map. It wasn't until several years later, during one of my hikes in Glacier, that I encountered a long-distance hiker who had a solar panel on the top of his backpack. When I asked him the purpose of the solar panel, he said he used it to charge his iPhone so he could use its GPS capabilities. I learned from him that you don't need to be within the range of a cell tower to use your iPhone's GPS capabilities. All it takes is the right GPS App and a power source to use your iPhone as a GPS device, even when you are off-grid. As soon as I returned from the Glacier hike, I purchased the appropriate GPS App and a battery pack that would last me for several days while on the trail. Now, when I am on a hike, if I get off the route, the GPS map will show me where I am and where the route is on the map. If I get off course, the GPS App can guide me back to the route. I would never go backpacking without a map, but the GPS App is a handy tool in addition to the map that would have instantly shown me that I was off course when hiking with Ashley and Brett.

Just as I wouldn't do a backpacking trip without the guidance that a map provides, I wouldn't do life without the guidance God's Word, the Bible, provides. Psalm 119:105 (NLT) tells us, "Your word is a lamp to guide my feet and a light for my path." The world without God's presence is void of light and engulfed in darkness. Genesis 1:3 tells us there was no physical light until God spoke it into existence. There is physical darkness without God, and at the same time, there is spiritual darkness without God. We are spiritually in darkness until our eyes open to God's presence. Reading the Bible daily will allow God to show us how to navigate through the darkness. This scripture is especially understandable to the backpacker who has hiked after dusk and is dependent on their headlamp to illuminate the path. It is a clear picture of how reliant we are on God to lead us spiritually through the darkness.

Not only do we have the Bible to guide us daily, but we also have His Holy Spirit. When you believe that Jesus died on the cross and rose from the dead and accept God's gift of forgiveness, a relationship is birthed between you and God. God's Holy Spirit then comes to live in you. 1 John 2:27 (NLT) tells us, "But you have received the Holy Spirit, and he lives within you, so you don't need anyone to teach you what is true. For the Spirit teaches you everything you need to know, and what he teaches is true—it is not a lie."

The Holy Spirit living in you will help you understand the Bible and speak to your heart to confirm what the Bible is saying. It is similar to the GPS and serves as a double-check for what we read in the Bible. We use our minds to read the Bible, but through His Holy Spirit, we are helped to understand what we are reading and how His Word comes alive in our hearts.

Reading the Bible daily is vital to having a relationship with God. The Bible is one way that God talks to us. God can also speak to us when we pray. Prayer involves talking to God and listening to God to direct our hearts. Reading the Bible and praying are critical parts of a relationship with God.

There are many ways to systematically read the Bible:

- *You can read it cover to cover*
- *You can follow a reading plan that tells you what scriptures to read each day*
- *You can pick individual scriptures and study them more deeply, along with a study guide*

I have enjoyed reading one Psalm, one Proverb, and one chapter from another book in the Bible each day, gradually working my way through the Bible. More recently, I read the Bible on an iPhone App, which has various reading plans available. Whatever method you choose, you should ask yourself this question about each passage you read—What is God saying to you through the scripture you read, and how can you apply it to your life? The Bible is your trail map as a believer and will help you navigate the path of life.

As Ashley, Brett, and I started to retrace our steps, we could hear the distant rumble of thunder. I found the turnoff I had missed, and we continued on the Loyalsock Trail heading towards Tamarack Run, where I wanted to camp for the night. The storm we heard earlier was getting closer, and we were behind schedule. Just one mile into our six-mile hike, I decided our best option was to set up camp quickly and wait out the storm.

There were no immediate areas to camp, so we settled right on the trail. Soon after the tents were set up, the skies opened, and the storm began. It was a significant storm, and I am glad we had the shelter of the tents to keep us dry. After about an hour, the storm moved on, and we could stretch out our legs and fill our water bottles in High Rock Run, which ran parallel to the trail. We ended up camping on the trail for the rest of the night. Our location did not lend itself to a campfire, so we had dinner and then headed to our tents to rest up for a 12-mile hike on Saturday since we had only hiked one mile on this day. I apologized to Ashley and Brett for our less-than-perfect day, but I was glad we were comfortable in our tents and could stay dry.

We packed up our tents in the morning and were hiking for just a few minutes when we discovered that we would have made it to a beautiful campsite next to High Rock Run if we had just hiked a little further the night before. Oh well, it was good for a laugh! I suggested to Ashley and Brett that we wait for breakfast at Alpine Falls, just a few miles from where we camped the night before. My first encounter with Alpine Falls was when Dave and I hiked the entire 59-mile length of the Loyalsock Trail a few years earlier. It was one of my all-time favorite backpacking experiences, as we walked in the fog at the end of a five-day backpacking trip, heading to our final night's destination. I shared with Ashley and Brett what a memorable experience I had at Alpine Falls as we had breakfast at the base. It is special to share old memories, especially as you create new ones.

We still had nine miles to hike, which took us by Tamarack Run, Sones Pond, and Loyalsock Creek. Immediately after crossing Loyalsock Creek, we turned off the Loyalsock Trail and went onto the Loyalsock Link Trail. After a few miles on the Loyalsock Link Trail, we came to Cold Run, which meant it was time to look for a campsite. Setting up camp is the highlight of each day for me, and I was glad to be able to share it with Ashley and Brett. We found a fine campsite next to Cold

Run, with a stone fire pit, a flat area for the tents, several seats formed out of large rocks, and plenty of firewood. We turned the spot into our temporary home, and I helped them prepare their dinner. I was glad Ashley and Brett got to experience the joys of a nice campsite after spending the previous night camped in the center of the trail.

After a peaceful night's sleep, we had breakfast around another fire, and then packed up camp and hiked the remaining three miles back to my SUV. This leg was an exceptionally pretty section of trail that crosses the West and East Branches of Double Run and several waterfalls. As far as backpacking, this trip was typical: a challenging climb, getting lost, changing plans when needed, creating memories, sitting by a campfire, and enjoying God's creation. The best part was sharing it with Ashley and Brett.

It was still early in the day when we returned to my SUV, and I suggested we go out for a post-hike meal. The post-hike meal is, without a doubt, the priority when you get off the trail. While trail food is enjoyed, appreciated, and sustaining, the post-hike meal is a celebration. It is a salute to accomplishing a goal, overcoming the challenges of the hike, and being back in civilization with those you just shared a backpacking experience with. It doesn't have to be any place special. A local dinner with the smell of bacon lingering in the air fits the bill; a steakhouse with raw meat to choose from is fantastic; a country buffet with an endless variety of food works as well. I suggested the Bullfrog Brewery in Williamsport, PA, which would be having its Sunday Brunch right about then. It was a 45-minute drive from the trailhead, and we would pass by Williamsport on our way home.

I was enthusiastically driving down an open stretch of highway when I saw the lights of a police cruiser approaching me from behind. I was pulled over, and I explained to the officer that we had just finished a three-day hike and were on our way out to eat. He examined my driver's license and insurance certificate, told me he would only give me a warning, and told me to slow down. While I was relieved I didn't get a ticket; it was humbling to be pulled over with Ashley and Brett in the car.

We continued to the Bullfrog Brewery, had a fantastic brunch, and continued our journey home. I was unfamiliar with the streets in Williamsport and ended up in the wrong lane when making a right-hand turn. Regardless, I made the turn and started to head towards the bridge that would take us over the river and out of town. Just then, I saw flashing lights behind me and realized I was being pulled over for the second time on the same day. I panicked because there was nowhere to pull off the road, so I continued to the other side of the river and immediately pulled into a parking lot.

I thought I was toast. For one thing, I was sure the warning I received just two hours earlier would be held over my head, plus I wasn't sure if my continuing to drive over the river was the right thing to do. When the officer approached my window, he asked, "Why didn't you pull over?" I explained that I didn't see anywhere I could safely pull over, so I waited until I got to the other side of the bridge. Then the officer said, "I should ticket you for turning from the wrong lane, but now that you are on the other side of the river you are out of my jurisdiction, and the paperwork I have to do is not worth writing the ticket." He told me to be safe and to continue my trip home.

Being pulled over once and given a warning is humbling. Being pulled over twice within two hours and not being ticketed is legendary! It reminded me that one of the best parts of doing a loop hike is riding with your fellow backpackers to and from the trailhead and then returning home!

Chapter Thirteen
GLACIER

At one point, Butch and I served on staff together at a church in Carlisle, Pennsylvania. As life evolved, I became the CEO of a construction company in Harrisburg, Pennsylvania. Butch landed in Spokane, Washington, as a Chaplain for a veterans' hospital. Butch started to explore the many backpacking opportunities in the Northwest and suggested we do a backpacking trip together in Glacier National Park, which is located about four hours east of Spokane in northern Montana.

In 1806, Lewis and Clark came within 50 miles of what is now Glacier National Park. By the mid-1800s, early settlers were exploring the area, and by 1891, the area became much more accessible when the Great Northern Railway was completed.[23] Glacier National Park was established as a national park in 1910, preserving one million acres of incredible natural resources for future generations. A glacier is a body of snow and ice that moves downhill as pulled by the forces of gravity. When the area was first explored, there were 150 active glaciers. At this time, only 25 remain.[24]

Several aspects of backpacking in Glacier impacted how I approached this excursion. I purchased maps and did internet research, but it was more complex than choosing where I wanted to hike and planning the trip. To preserve the natural resources, the park service manages the backpacking and hiking opportunities to protect them from excessive use. Day hikes are relatively easy to plan and do, but if you want to stay on the trail overnight, it is much more regulated.

Staying in the wilderness overnight is called being in the "backcountry." To stay in the backcountry, you need a backcountry permit. About half of the backcountry permits are issued in advance online and are usually snatched up early in the year. The remaining permits are issued in person the day before or the morning of your hike. It was later in the summer when our plan took shape, and by then, all of the permits issued in advance were taken. We would have to see what was available when we got to the park. Regardless, I still had to choose several trips that were the right length and within our hiking capabilities, knowing that I might not get my first or second choice since they were distributed on a first-come, first-serve basis.

Another thing I had to research and plan for was carrying a bear canister and bear spray. The black bear and grizzly

---

[23]"Early Settlers." NPS Glacier National Park Montana, www.nps.gov/glac/learn/historyculture/early-settlers.htm (February 27, 2023).
[24]Eric Molvar, *Hiking Glacier and Waterton Lakes National Parks*, (Helena, MT: Globe Pequot Press, 2012), 1,3.

bear population is thriving in Glacier. Carrying a bear canister is required in this national park since not all campsites have food hanging stations. There is an approved list of bear canisters allowed by the park, with specific canisters not being on the list because they proved ineffective once the bear population figured out how to open them. The goal of a bear canister is not to safeguard your food from a bear stealing it (aka Yogi Bear) but rather to keep the bear from getting a taste for human food. Once a bear is exposed to human food, they will seek out humans for the food they carry. It is also recommended that you carry bear spray in Glacier.

Lastly, I had to plan my flight to Washington and determine how to get the backpacking equipment to my destination. I was concerned about checking my backpacking equipment as luggage with the airlines because it could get lost in transit. I decided instead to ship my equipment to Butch's house several weeks in advance of our hike. That way, I knew my equipment would be there waiting for me. On a subsequent trip, I checked my equipment as luggage and crossed my fingers that it would make it there with me—which it did.

Whether you take your equipment with you on the flight or ship it to your destination ahead of time, there are some items that you will have to purchase once you arrive. There are restrictions on shipping and packing items such as batteries, stove fuel, and bear spray. As soon as you arrive at your destination, you will need to seek out these items to have them for your hike. The downside is that you may have to pay a premium for these items in a remote location; the upside is that it gives you a legitimate excuse to spend some time in a backpacking store to see what equipment is popular in another part of the country.

I arrived in Spokane, Washington, on a Thursday early in September. Once back at Butch's home, I unpacked the shipping boxes and prepared for our hike the best I could. At this point, we had a general idea of where we wanted to hike but needed a specific itinerary. On Friday morning, we drove east for four hours to the western entrance of Glacier. We then drove the 50-mile-long Going-to-the-Sun Road on our way to our final destination: the Many Glacier Campground. It was a two-hour drive from when we first entered the park to the campground, and it revealed the diversity and size of this vast national park. Once at the Many Glacier Campground, we set up a base camp using Butch's four-man tent and then headed to the Ranger Station to set our itinerary for the rest of our trip.

We were thoroughly impressed with how helpful and knowledgeable the staff at the Ranger Station was. Once it was our turn, we described our experience level and the type of backcountry trip we hoped to plan. I then shared my first preference, but when they checked, no backcountry camping sites were available. The ranger saw my countenance drop and said, "No worries, there are no bad hikes in Glacier!" I shared my second preference, and sites were available, so we purchased the permits for two nights in the backcountry.

The next step was to watch a backcountry video that instructed us on low-impact backpacking and how to handle an encounter with a bear. The last step was a one-on-one meeting with a park ranger who reviewed our itinerary with us. He had specific guidance about the trails we would be hiking and then instructed us on using the bear spray. He reinforced some of the instructions presented in the video. Then he added, "Don't use the whole can of spray on the first bear." It was meant to be reassuring that it doesn't take a lot of spray to deter a bear, but I couldn't help but interpret it as a caution that we may have more than one bear encounter. We left the Ranger Station feeling confident and reassured that this would be an amazing trip.

It was still early afternoon, and we had picked out a few day hikes in advance that we could do in this area. We decided to hike to Cracker Lake, a six-mile hike following Canyon Creek. I am so glad we made the effort to get on the trail during our first day in the park. I am not a big fan of campground camping; this was a way to make something out of our long day of driving and preparing for our backcountry trip. On our way to Cracker Lake, we encountered a few hikers returning from our destination who shared that there was a grizzly bear at the base of the mountain on the opposite side of the lake and a moose hidden in the brush along the edge of the lake. Our anticipation and pace picked up as we made our way on the trail.

The trail climbed slightly as it approached Cracker Lake, and you could only see the lake once you reached the summit. Suddenly, you were looking down into the lake in front of you about 200 yards below. Another group of hikers gazed down into the lake, and we asked them if they had seen the grizzly bear or moose. They pointed to where they were told the grizzly bear had been seen but had not seen it themselves. They then pointed to where the moose was and explained that you had to get closer to see it. The group descended from sight on the trail, and we had Cracker Lake to ourselves.

There was a quiet stillness in the scene. It was beyond tranquil and had a hallowed feeling to it. It was as if we had walked to the edge of God's creation and looked down into another world. The water in the lake was turquoise, and although I had seen pictures of glacial lakes before, I saw them almost in disbelief, thinking that the photo was slightly altered. Until you see it in person, it seems less than authentic.

There were pockets of snow in the mountain on the other side of the lake that remained from the prior winter. There is a vastness in the landscape that I came to appreciate at Glacier.

The mountains, valleys, and lakes are all so massive. On one hand, the land features look like they are right in front of you, but as you begin to walk towards them, you realize how much further away from you they are than what you thought. The size of the land features gives you the illusion that they are closer than they are.

We went to the shore of the lake, across from where the moose reportedly was, but we couldn't see it. Butch had his camera with a telephoto lens and, with the help of the camera, was able to locate the moose. Imagine an animal the size of a moose lost in the weeds on the edge of a lake. This view again showed us the vastness of the landscape.

We reverently walked around a portion of the lake and took some photos. Butch commented that there was no way that an image could capture what we were experiencing, and I agreed. We hiked the six miles back to Butch's car at the trailhead and drove back to our base camp as the sun was setting. We now had a taste of what we would experience over the next three days and headed to the tent to rest up for our journey.

Our permits created a 26-mile loop starting and ending at the Many Glacier Campground. On Friday, we would hike six miles on the Redgap Pass Trail and camp at Poia Lake. On Saturday we would hike an additional ten miles on the Redgap Pass Trail and camp at Elizabeth Lake. On Sunday, we would hike ten miles on the Ptarmigan Trail, which would take us back to the Many Glacier Campground.

The trail to Poia Lake was well marked and maintained, as were all the trails we were on in Glacier. The backcountry campsite had a food hanging station, a food prep area, a pit toilet, and four pads to pitch tents on. Each tent pad was designed to hold two tents for a maximum of four people. Thus, this campsite could have a maximum of sixteen people spread around a reasonably large area of the lake. We only encountered others at the food prep area and never felt the number of people at the site impacted the experience. There was a lot of signage explaining the guidelines for staying at the site, and it was a highly regulated environment. It did feel a little sterile, but I understand why it had to be this way. If the park were not correctly managed, it would not be preserved for future generations. I appreciate the steps to safeguard the environment and experience such an incredible place.

Once we had our tents set up and had dinner, we explored the area a little. We crossed a footbridge over Kennedy Creek that flowed out of Poia Lake and followed a side trail to a summit that overlooked Poia Lake. From that vantage point, we had a view of Poia Lake, a large waterfall where Kennedy Creek began, and Redgap Pass, where we would be hiking the following day. We stayed there until the sun began to set, and the view was spectacular!

The next day, we followed Kennedy Creek for several miles and then climbed 1,500 feet in less than three miles to Redgap Pass at an elevation of 7,500 feet. We were now surrounded by spiraling mountain peaks dressed in hues of sand, red, gray, and green, with many topped off by snow-capped peaks. This view was the highlight of the day for me, with the vastness and massiveness of the mountain range stretching in every direction as far as you could see.

We caught our physical and emotional breath and then began the 2,500-foot descent over the next four miles. We could see Elizabeth Lake from the Redgap Pass several hours before we would stand at its shoreline. When we first saw Elizabeth Lake, what looked like a small, quiet lake turned out to be an impressively vast body of water with mini-white capped waves that lapped the shoreline. Elizabeth Lake had two backcountry campsites. Our permits were for the site at the foot of the lake, which had five tent pads. The setup was very similar to the site at Poia Lake, and we set up camp for the night.

Belly River flowed out of Elizabeth Lake and had the look and familiarity of the streams I fly fished in Pennsylvania. This backpacking trip was one of the few that I packed a fly rod for. I put on my swim trunks and sandals and waded and fished for an hour or so without any action. Honestly, I was so preoccupied with the thought of encountering a bear while I was fishing that I really couldn't relax and enjoy myself. We napped on the lake's shoreline, had dinner, and then turned in for the night.

The following day, as we were packing up our camp, a bull moose strolled through our campsite, crossed Belly River, and continued up the side of the mountain. We got some great photos, which made for an exciting start to the day. We passed the moose again about an hour later as we climbed out of the valley on the Ptarmigan Trail.

Throughout the morning, there was significant fog and cloud cover in the valley as we climbed 2,500 feet towards the Ptarmigan Tunnel. There was very low visibility, and the sun could not be seen. As we were making the climb, a park ranger came up from behind us with a warning that a major storm was approaching and several inches of snow were expected. It was reassuring to know that although we were in a remote and mountainous area, park rangers were on patrol to watch for our safety. We reached the Ptarmigan Tunnel, a 240-foot underground passage cut through the mountain rock as a travel path for horses and foot traffic. On the other side of the tunnel, it was a sunny day with no cloud cover. You could see and experience the impact that the mountains have on the movement of a weather system. We began the 2,400-foot descent that would take us back to the Many Glacier Campground and saw mountain goats at several locations throughout the rest of the day.

If I had to choose one word to describe what I saw and experienced in Glacier, it would be "vast." You can't help but see God's creative hand in the diversity and size of Glacier's mountains, meadows, lakes, streams, wildlife, and weather.

Psalms 104:24-25 (NLT) proclaims, "O Lord, what a variety of things you have made! In wisdom you have made them all. The earth is full of your creatures. Here is the ocean, vast and wide, teeming with life of every kind, both large and small." I have said that I feel closest to God in the wilderness backpacking. That sense was even greater at Glacier and was compounded by the variety and vastness of his creation that was all around us.

The vastness of God's creation is beyond our imagination or understanding. We are on a small planet, just the proper distance from the sun, which is part of the Milky Way Galaxy. There are 100 billion stars in the Milky Way galaxy and an estimated 140 billion galaxies in the universe.[25] This is the physical dimension of creation, of which we have firsthand, although very limited, experience.

Our understanding of the spiritual dimension of creation is even more limited. It includes realities described in the Bible, such as angels, demons, the ability for humans to be translated from one physical location to another,

---

[25] Bill Bryson, *A Short History of Nearly Everything* (New York, NY: Broadway Books, 2003), 27.

individuals being brought back from the dead, and other miracles that clearly break the laws of the physical dimension that we think we understand and live in.

Not only am I in awe of God as I consider the creation we are currently a part of, but our final eternal destination of heaven is beyond my comprehension. One of the descriptions of heaven is found in Revelation 21:21 (NLT), where it describes, "The twelve gates were made of pearls—each gate from a single pearl! And the main street was pure gold, as clear as glass."

Now consider that the God who created all of this knows you by name and desires to have a relationship with you. When I see the vastness of his creation, I realize how fortunate I am to know God and to be able to fellowship with the creator of the universe! Always treasure your relationship with God as he walks with you on the path of life.

This trip had many memorable backpacking experiences for me: the day hike to Cracker Lake and seeing my first glacial lake and moose in the wild, the evening spent exploring Poia Lake as the sun set on the horizon, the beauty of the spiraling mountain peaks at Redgap Pass, the descent to Elizabeth Lake, fly fishing in Belly River, the climb up the foggy Ptarmigan Trail and seeing the weather change on the other side of the Ptarmigan Tunnel, and experiencing God's vast creation with my hiking buddy Butch.

Our original plan was to spend the night at the campground and do another day hike on Monday, but because of the approaching storm, we decided to cut our trip a day short and head back to Butch's house. As we left the park and pondered our experience, we agreed with what the park ranger said, "There are no bad hikes in Glacier"!

Chapter Fourteen
THE BUCKET LIST

I was never a big fan of the whole social media craze. However, I made one random post on Mark's LinkedIn account, leading to our meeting for coffee. The construction company I worked for had some human resource management needs, and Mark was a human resource consultant.

As we drank our coffee and chatted, it became apparent that although the reason for our meeting was business, the focus became our shared passion for backpacking. We both had similar backpacking experiences and lost 40 pounds to make hiking easier. During our conversation, Mark shared that one item on his bucket list was a winter hike to one of the Appalachian Mountain Club (AMC) huts in the White Mountains of New Hampshire.

Backpacking & the Path of Life

The Appalachian Trail (AT) crosses through the White Mountains, and the AMC has a hut system that allows backpackers to navigate between them to traverse the challenging terrain. Most of the trails and huts are closed during the winter, but several remain open year-round for cross-country skiers and winter backpackers. Mark dreamed of hiking to one of these huts during winter.

Neither of us had ever backpacked in winter, but after reflecting on our meeting and researching, I told Mark I was game to help him check this item off his bucket list. We explored what the hike would entail and purchased additional equipment: a winter sleeping bag, microspikes for hiking on ice, snowshoes for hiking in snow, and winter clothing such as thermal underwear, down gloves, and a compact down jacket.

To test our new gear and get a feel for winter backpacking, we decided on a local hike—a 16-mile stretch of the AT in Pennsylvania from Clarks Creek to the Susquehanna River. Mark and I had met for coffee in October, and we planned this "practice" hike three months later in January.

This dry run also allowed us to get to know each other better and determine if we were compatible hiking partners. When spending several days on the trail with someone, it's essential to gauge compatibility regarding physical abilities, hiking pace, and problem-solving skills when unexpected situations arise.

We began on a Friday, reaching the Peter Mountain Shelter for our first night on the trail. Packed ice on the trail allowed us to test our microspikes, but we didn't need our snowshoes because it rained on Saturday morning, prompting us to wait it out at the shelter. Spending the entire day there was beneficial, allowing Mark and me to develop our friendship.

During our stay at Peter Mountain Shelter, an unexpected visitor arrived under an umbrella, looking unlike the typical hiker. We invited him into the shelter, and I offered him a cup of coffee. He accepted and explained that walking the trail was part of his daily recovery routine after nearly dying from hepatitis. After finishing his coffee, he continued on his way. I cleaned my coffee cup thoroughly with boiled water before my next cup!

Other than this encounter, the hike was pretty uneventful. We spent two nights at Peter Mountain Shelter and, on Sunday, hiked the remaining miles back to our vehicle parked at the mountain's base. We tested some of our winter gear and found that we were indeed compatible hiking partners. We still needed an opportunity to use our snowshoes, which would come later.

Since we had just hiked the AT and were near Duncannon, having a post-hike meal at the Doyle Hotel seemed fitting. The AT passes close to the Doyle Hotel, a traditional resting place for thru-hikers from Georgia to Maine. The Doyle is renowned more for tradition than luxury accommodations. I remember enjoying an excellent hamburger and fries while Mark remarked, "You should write a book." I shrugged and replied, "You never know!" It was a worthwhile goal to add to my bucket list.

Over the next year, plans for a March hike to Carter Notch Hut took shape. We tested our snowshoes weeks before when a snowstorm dumped a foot of snow in Mark's familiar area of Northern PA. Spending the day learning to hike with snowshoes was invaluable preparation for our March hike.

We arrived at White Mountain National Forest on a Sunday and stayed our first night at Joe Dodge Lodge, a hub for outdoor activities. The lodge offered heated rooms, showers, and a dining hall. Unaware of the meeting of teams for Kate Matrosova's search and rescue, we went to the dining hall for dinner. The teams had recently participated in the search for

Kate Matrosova, who tragically passed away a month before our visit. Their focus was on assessing coordination for future rescue efforts.

An experienced hiker, Kate planned to hike four mountains named after American Presidents in the White Mountains on Presidents Day. It would be a 15-mile hike with an early morning temperature of -5°F and 45 mph winds. For someone of her experience, this was a reasonable safe hike. Conditions change quickly in the White Mountains, and suddenly she was faced with -20°F with 100 mph winds.[26] Her body was found the next day off the trail, the 156th victim of the White Mountains since 1849.[27] Though we wouldn't climb to the altitude Kate attempted, her story reinforced the importance of safety and not pushing limits.

On Monday morning, we geared up and headed south on the AT for a five-mile hike to Carter Notch Hut. The snow-covered forest was breathtaking, and using snowshoes was surprisingly easy. A packed snow trail made it easier to cover ground than on rock and log-covered terrain. Trail blazes a foot above the snow indicate five to six feet of packed snow under our snowshoes.

We reached the hut in good time, settled into the bunkhouse, and hiked the Wildcat River Trail in the afternoon without our packs. Returning to the bunkhouse, we retrieved our food and then went to the main hut to prepare our dinner. The main hut included a kitchen, dining area, wood stove, and caretaker's room. The weekend crowd had departed, leaving a few local hikers and the caretaker.

---

[26] Ty Gagne, *Where You'll Find Me: Risk, Decisions, and the Last Climb of Kate Matrosova* (Conway, NH: TMC Books LLC, 2017), 2,34,37.
[27] "List of People who died on the Presidential Range." Wikipedia, en.wikipedia.org/wiki/List_of_people_who_died_on_the_Presidential_Range (February 27, 2023).

The Bucket List

While preparing food, I overheard local hikers discussing past experiences, including sliding down various mountains, sometimes covering up to a third of a mile. Intrigued, I asked if they were serious about sliding down mountains, and they confirmed it, explaining how they cover the bottom of their pants with duct tape for the descent—a common practice, though new to me.

We headed to the unheated bunkhouse for the night. The air temperature was in the low teens, but I was very comfortable in my zero-degree-rated sleeping bag. I slept well and bravely got out of my sleeping bag in the morning to head to the main hut for breakfast.

After breakfast, we did a day hike to the summit of Carter Dome, which stands at 4,833 feet in elevation. The freedom of carrying just a day pack made for an awesome hike. The summit of Carter Dome was the highlight of our hike as we gazed at the imposing Mount Washington about six miles away. Mount Washington, at 6,288 feet, is the highest peak in the northeast and holds one of the world's highest recorded wind velocities at 231 miles per hour.[28] Mark and I considered continuing along the trail past the summit, but the wind was picking up at this altitude, and the deep snowpack had covered most of the trail markers. We decided not to push our limits and headed back to the hut.

Sections of the trail were rather steep, making hiking down them almost impossible. What do you do when the trail is too steep and slippery to hike? You take off your snowshoes, sit on your butt, and slide! This approach was hilariously fun with an element of danger because stopping required careful planning. Our technique involved lining up behind trees on the

---

[28] "Wind Speed." Wikipedia, en.wikipedia.org/wiki/Windspeed (February 27, 2023).

trail and "sliding" short distances from one tree to the next. It was easy to see why this had become a mode of entertainment for local hikers—it was a blast!

It was a thrill helping Mark check this hike off his bucket list. It was also sobering to consider that Kate Matrosova might have had a similar bucket list, perhaps including hiking the Presidential Range on Presidents Day. We can't live in fear of what "could happen," but at the same time, we must know our limits and use wisdom on the trail.

Bucket lists and goals are good because they push us to get the most out of life. But the most valuable item on your bucket list is fulfilling God's purpose for your life. Once we fulfill God's purpose, our ultimate reward is living eternally with Him. The Apostle Paul shares in Philippians 3:14 (NLT): "I press on to reach the end of the race and receive the heavenly prize for which God, through Christ Jesus, is calling us."

We are all at different stages of the race that Paul describes. Some are nearing life's end, while others have yet to begin. As a children's pastor, I prayed with many children who started this race while still in elementary school. The race begins when you realize you were born with a sinful nature and need forgiveness. We may try to earn this forgiveness but always fall short because we are human. Then we learn forgiveness is a gift from God, not earned by being good.

This gift became available when God became flesh in Jesus, taking the punishment for our sins. When you believe Jesus died on the cross to pay for your sins and rose from the dead, you receive the gift of forgiveness and eternal life. This is where your race begins.

As believers, we've begun this race, pressing on for the prize of heaven. We run in this race daily. The most important part is developing a personal relationship with God. This involves reading the Bible, through which God guides and speaks to us, and praying—a two-way conversation. We listen for His guidance and comfort as we share our hearts with God.

We encounter difficulties or even fall during this race, but we press on, asking God for help overcoming or enduring them. Each struggle reveals God's presence, strengthening our faith and using us in ways we'd never imagined.

Years pass, and we reach advanced age, passing from this life to the next. Our bodies die, but our spirits live on, receiving the promised heavenly prize. Following the path of life, we can now live eternally with God. This future is the ultimate item on your bucket list!

Safely back at Carter Notch Hut, we spent another chilly night in the bunkhouse. We snowshoed five miles back to the lodge on Monday morning, retrieved our car, and headed home. Two years later, we returned to the White Mountains, this time to Lonesome Lake Hut. For the second trip, we had our own "sliding" stories!

Chapter Fifteen
OLD LOGGERS PATH

I am not going to say that the Old Loggers Path is my favorite to backpack, but the trail has several qualities that make it memorable to me. I met a fellow named Max at a business meeting once, and when we discovered that we shared a passion for backpacking, we struck up the typical conversation that goes something like this: "What backpack do you use? Do you prefer a tent or a hammock? How do you filter your water? Do you have any favorite trail meals? What trails do you enjoy?" It's always enriching to pick someone's brain about backpacking; you never know what information will be helpful on a future hike. What stuck in my memory was Max's exclusive preference for backpacking on the Old Loggers Path in Lycoming County, Pennsylvania—it was hands down his favorite trail.

There are several reasons why this 27-mile loop trail is excellent for backpacking. Loop trails are convenient since you only need one vehicle parked at the trailhead to complete the hike. My preferred way to backpack this loop is to park at the Masten trailhead and hike clockwise. On the first day, you hike eleven miles and camp at Pleasant Stream. On the second day, you hike another eleven miles and camp at what I call the "hidden gem" campsite, a beautiful spot along spectacular Rock Run. This setup is motivational because it gives you something to anticipate throughout the hike.

During the challenging stretches, you remind yourself of the beautiful campsite waiting for you at Rock Run—and every time, it exceeds expectations. The final day of the loop is an easy five-mile hike on level terrain back to your vehicle.

The only drawback I have found with the Old Loggers Path is its popularity, which attracts more backpackers each time I visit. I hesitate to share this story, knowing it might draw an even larger crowd!

My first hike on the Old Loggers Path was with Pastor Lee, whom I served with as a children's pastor in Carlisle, Pennsylvania. This was several years after our time on staff together and a year after he climbed Mount Kilimanjaro as part of a fundraiser for clean water wells in Africa. This trip gave us time to catch up and for me to hear about his climb.

Lee started backpacking a few years after we worked together. He decided to try backpacking, bought the necessary gear, and learned the ropes through trial and error. He had some amusing stories from his early backpacking attempts, and his approach was still somewhat unconventional.

This hike occurred in March, starting on a Friday and concluding on Sunday. The parking lot at the Masten trailhead was closed due to a construction project, so we parked on Yellow Dog Road, where the trail intersects. We hiked counter-clockwise, spending our first night along Pleasant Stream after a 10-mile hike. One unique thing Lee does is set up a hammock and a tent at camp. He graciously brought a second hammock for me to try out. He explained that he likes to nap once camp is set up, and it sounded like a great idea, so I joined him. The nap was rejuvenating, and I started considering getting a hammock for future trips.

While lounging around camp that evening, a porcupine casually wandered through our campsite. The animal seemed unfazed by our presence as it ambled by. I've had several encounters with wildlife passing close to or through a campsite before. Once in Dolly Sods, a herd of whitetail deer spent the evening in the woods around us while we sat by the campfire. On another occasion, a large black bear wandered uncomfortably close to our campsite on the Quehanna Trail. In Montana, I woke to find a bull moose strolling through our campsite, munching on tree leaves. It's always a special treat to witness wildlife in its natural habitat.

We hiked 11 miles on Saturday and camped at Hoghouse Run, where we again took a nap before preparing and enjoying our dinner. Our plan for Sunday was to hike the remaining six miles back to our vehicle. We covered about four miles when we reached Rock Run. I had read about how beautiful the stream was, but the descriptions did not do it justice. Rock Run has a strong current and has carved a deep gorge through the mountain rock. The trail follows the stream for about a mile, and the scenery is breathtaking. There are multiple waterfalls, white-capped rapids, overhanging ledges, and deep pools—all under a canopy of hemlocks, rhododendrons, and mountain laurels. It's a stunning area, and I knew I would return.

Two years later, I did return for a late June hike with my hiking buddy, Mark. We started on a Friday and hiked through Sunday. Now, in summer, I got to experience the area with leaves on the trees but also faced the challenge of walking the mountains in the summer heat.

We parked at the Masten trailhead and hiked clockwise for 11 miles to Pleasant Stream, where we spent our first night on the trail. On Saturday, we planned to hike another 11 miles to Rock Run. Earlier, I had told Mark about the beauty of Rock Run and how I was looking forward to camping beside it. As we ascended an area marked on the map as Big Rocks and took our final steps onto the summit, we were startled by a loud, distinct hissing and rattling sound. We soon realized that the trail led us to a rock overhang with several large rattlesnakes underneath—it was indeed a rattlesnake den. We managed to snap a few photos from a safe distance.

Arriving at Rock Run was even more spectacular and dramatic than I remembered. Several streams converge here, cascading into Rock Run over waterfalls. Over years of relentless flow, the water has carved through solid mountain rock, creating a breathtaking sight. We followed the trail along Rock Run in search of a campsite but couldn't find an established spot for the night. When the trail started to veer away from the creek, we stumbled upon a suitable campsite. Although it wasn't right by the stream, we were close enough to catch glimpses of the water through the trees. I was a bit disappointed not to be closer to the stream, and after setting up camp, we had to navigate a 40-foot descent down a steep hillside, moving from tree to tree to keep our footing while descending to the stream so that we could fetch some water.

While exploring the area by the stream, I stumbled upon the best campsite I have ever seen. It featured a sizable fire pit constructed from large rocks, with rock chairs around it—a large stone for seating and another for back support. Several other tables and features were also crafted from stones. Someone had invested considerable time and effort to create this hidden gem along Rock Run. Adjacent to the campsite was a pool of water carved into the rock. I took the opportunity to rinse off in the pool, cooling down and freshening up after a hot and challenging day on the trail. Although our camp was already set for the night, I noted a landmark along the trail that would help me find this spot again.

On Sunday, Mark and I hiked the remaining five miles of the loop back to my SUV parked at the Masten trailhead. I noticed how easy the hiking was that morning and realized what a great hike it would be for Cindy to join me.

I returned to Rock Run with Cindy over the next two summers. We parked my SUV at the Masten trailhead and hiked the easy five miles to Rock Run. We camped at the same site where Mark and I had stayed, as the hike to the hidden gem along the stream would have been too tricky for Cindy. When Cindy and I visited Rock Run, we explored different areas along the beautiful stream. The second time, we went for my birthday, and Cindy packed a cupcake and candle to celebrate—it was a perfect birthday present!

Until now, I had not yet had the chance to spend a night at the streamside campsite that I described as the hidden gem along Rock Run. I wanted to change that when I planned a hike with my son-in-law Steve and his friend Matt. Matt, Steve's high school friend who had recently returned from military service, was an experienced backpacker. A year after our hike, Matt attempted a thru-hike on the Appalachian Trail, starting at Springer Mountain, Georgia, and making it as far as New York before spraining his ankle.

Steve, Matt, and I came from different states and met at the Masten trailhead. We started the hike on a Thursday in May, hiking the trail clockwise and camping our first night along Pleasant Stream. I told Steve and Matt about camping at the hidden gem on Friday night and the special treat awaiting us. Unlike the encounter Mark and I had with rattlesnakes at Big Rocks, we encountered none, likely due to the time of year. Upon arriving at Rock Run, I was again surprised at its beauty.

We passed the confluence of streams and waterfalls, continuing along Rock Run on the Old Loggers Path. It was a day of typical ascents and descents, and after 11 miles of hiking, we were all ready to set up camp and recuperate. I began searching for the landmark I had found years earlier to leave the trail and find the hidden gem campsite. The trail started veering away from Rock Run, and I realized I had hiked too far and missed the landmark. We turned back, retracing our steps in the opposite direction, still searching for the landmark.

Once again, I realized we had passed it without noticing. Feeling foolish, I apologized to Steve and Matt for the extra hiking we had to do. We continued following the trail parallel to Rock Run, again unable to find the landmark. We retraced our steps until finally, after passing the landmark three times, I located it. I am unsure how many times I would have searched before giving up and settling for the easier-access campsite I had used before—I can be pretty persistent, and it might have taken several more trips back and forth on that trail before giving up.

Jesus tells a parable about persistence in prayer in Luke 11. The parable describes someone who had no food at home when a friend unexpectedly visited in the middle of the night. Wanting to feed his friend, he went to a neighbor's house to ask for bread. The neighbor, already in bed, initially refused but eventually gave in due to the persistent knocking. Jesus uses this illustration to instruct us on prayer in Luke 11:9-10 (NLT): "And so I tell you, keep on asking, and you will receive what you ask for. Keep on seeking, and you will find. Keep on knocking, and the door will be opened to you. For everyone who asks, receives. Everyone who seeks, finds. And to everyone who knocks, the door will be opened."

Do you have a need? God wants you to ask Him for help each day in prayer persistently. Whether it's a sin you struggle with or healing you need in your body, God invites you to ask persistently for His intervention. While there are instances in the Bible where God answered prayers immediately, more often, persistent prayer demonstrates faith and trust in Him. God's timing may differ from ours, and you never know what He is orchestrating behind the scenes while you await an answer to prayer.

Effective persistence in prayer requires daily communion with God. He desires a relationship with us, necessitating regular interaction. Here's what it looks like: I set my alarm 45 minutes earlier each morning to prepare for work. My day begins with a cup of coffee Cindy prepared the night before. Finding a quiet spot, currently my living room sofa, since it's just Cindy and me at home, I begin with reading the Bible. I reflect on how the scripture applies to my life at this moment. The remaining time is spent in prayer, following a format similar to the Lord's Prayer found in Luke 11:2-4. This passage guides believers on prayer.

I acknowledge God, often saying, "Good morning, God! You are great and awesome!" Confession follows to clear any barriers between us: "As you know, I lost my temper at work yesterday. Please forgive me and help me do better today." Also, forgiveness toward others is crucial, mirroring God's forgiveness toward us. Gratitude comes next, a lengthy list of recent and long-past blessings. Lastly, I present my requests to God, reminding Him of my persisting needs.

Your prayer is a two-way conversation with God and He needs an opportunity to speak as well. Take some time to simply be still, quiet, and wait on God to speak to your heart. Prayer needn't be elaborate—it's a conversation with a friend. Are you persistently praying daily as you journey on the path of life?

The landmark on the trail matched my memory, leading us to Rock Run's hidden gem. Once we arrived, Steve and Matt understood my persistence. We pitched tents and gathered firewood, enjoying an incredible evening fire with luxury seating around the fire pit.

While I won't declare the Old Loggers Path my favorite backpacking trail, the hidden gem is undoubtedly my favorite camping site. Before departing that morning, I marked the hidden gem's GPS location. You might wonder about the landmark or GPS coordinates—I wish I could provide them, but be persistent and you will find it!

Chapter Sixteen
SPRING SURPRISE

It was in the middle of winter, and this was a good project since I didn't have any hikes planned yet for the upcoming year. The maps were laid out all over the basement floor, and I finished waterproofing the last one. These were trail maps that I mail-ordered from the Pennsylvania Department of Conservation and Natural Resources (DCNR); unfortunately, they were not waterproofed.

My task for the evening was to paint them with map sealer to protect them from the elements. They were a little stiff once sealed and made them even harder to fold than normal. Once the maps were sealed, I used a map measuring tool to help me mark the trails with mileage markers as an aid when using them for backpacking. Pennsylvania has an impressive list of State Parks and State Forest lands, many of which have hiking trails passing through them. The DCNR used to make these paper maps available only by mail, but now, the maps are accessible online as PDF files.

I ended up hiking several trails shown on the maps, but the one that caught my eye first was the Pinchot Trail in Lackawanna State Forest. I needed an easy trail to take Cindy hiking on, and this trail looked promising. It is a 24-mile loop with a road running through its center so that you can hike the 11-mile northern section or the 13-mile southern section. I decided to backpack the 24-mile loop before taking Cindy on it to determine what part of the trail would work best for us later in the year. Even when others rate a trail as "easy," I didn't want to chance their definition of "easy" being different from mine. I wanted to pre-hike it to ensure it was a trail Cindy would feel comfortable on.

I decided to hike it solo, knowing it wouldn't be much more than a casual walk in the woods for my other hiking buddies. While I enjoy the camaraderie of hiking with others, there are some aspects of solo hiking that I enjoy every once in a while. Solo hiking allows me to be alone with my thoughts and focus on my personal goals or challenges. Also, I appreciate the feeling that I can take care of myself alone in the woods. I am no Daniel Boone, but it is nice to know that I could survive a few nights in the woods if I ever had to.

It was a Friday in March when I drove for this hike two hours north to the Wilkes-Barre area of Pennsylvania. It was my first spring hike, even though the calendar indicated that spring was still a few weeks away. Looking at the map, major highways completely surrounded the trail system, and I wondered if it would even feel like I was in the woods. However, once I arrived, the trail had a remote feel, with diverse woodlands, streams, wetlands, and a large pond. Moreover, I was

Spring Surprise

the only car at the trailhead, and I didn't encounter another person on the trail the entire weekend.

It was a 12-mile hike to Choke Creek, my destination for the night. The reasonably flat terrain made it an "easy" hike, but I maintained a quick pace. When you hear a trail rated as "easy," you tend to forget that you are carrying 30 pounds on your back, so describing any hike as "easy" becomes a relative description. Nonetheless, it was a good workout, and it felt great to be back on the trail after a long winter.

I was pleasantly surprised by the size and beauty of Choke Creek. If I had brought my fly rod, I would have enjoyed fishing for some of its wild brook trout. The trail system prohibits open fires from March through May. While I was a little disappointed that I couldn't have a fire to enjoy with my dinner, it relieved me of the pressure to gather firewood and ensure the fire was properly extinguished before bedtime. I had my dinner without the company or warmth of a fire and then headed to bed with plans to rise early to complete the remaining 12 miles of trail on Saturday.

I slept soundly and woke to an eerily quiet sensation. As I emerged from my tent, I couldn't believe my eyes—two inches of snow had fallen overnight. This surprise was completely unexpected and made for a beautiful hike for the rest of the day. It was a heavy, wet snow that coated the trees and landscape. It was a simple thing but made for one of my favorite backpacking memories. If I had known about the impending snow shower, I probably would have stayed home, not wanting to risk driving on snowy roads. A day or two after the snowfall, the snow would have been packed and mixed with mud. However, waking up to snow without expecting it and being alone in the woods to make the first footprints was extraordinary.

I completed the remainder of the hike and decided the northern section would be best for Cindy. When I returned home, I eagerly showed Cindy the snowy scene I had awakened to earlier that day, and she agreed that it looked like a beautiful area for hiking. Cindy and I returned to the Pinchot Trail in September for the hike, and we spent the night camping along Painter Creek, a creek in the northern section of the loop.

I had another spring surprise on an April hike with co-workers Denny and Tom, Tom's son Trent, and our company's HR consultant, Mark. This was a 29-mile hike on the Appalachian Trail (AT), starting at the Clarks Creek trailhead and heading north. Mark and I had hiked the AT starting at the same point and heading south two years earlier, part of our ongoing desire to hike the Pennsylvania AT from the Maryland border to the New Jersey border. We planned to hike 11 miles on Friday from Clarks Creek to Rausch Creek, 13 miles on Saturday to the William Penn Shelter, and 5 miles on Sunday to our vehicle, which we had shuttled to a parking lot on Route 501 where it intersects the trail.

The Clarks Creek trailhead is a quick 20-minute drive from Harrisburg, Pennsylvania's capital. Surprisingly, such a remote and rich wilderness is so convenient to a major population center. The area boasts Clarks Creek and Stoney Creek, both excellent trout streams where I've encountered wild turkeys, black bears, deer, rattlesnakes, and even a bobcat while fly fishing.

Another intriguing aspect of the area is its history: once a thriving community of over 1,000 people in the late 1800s and early 1900s known as the Village of Rausch Gap. It had a coal mining industry and serviced the railroad's equipment repairs. When the mines ceased production and the railroad operations moved, the community dwindled, leaving remnants like

Spring Surprise

building foundations, abandoned roads, mining equipment, and an old cemetery.[29] Access roads have disappeared, leaving foot travel as the only means to explore the area.

As typical of the AT, our trail began with a 1,000-foot climb to the top of Sharp Mountain, where it remained for the rest of the day. During our ascent, we encountered an AT thru-hiker who had started at Springer Mountain, Georgia, in January. Typically, thru-hikers begin in Georgia in March, following the emergence of Spring and Summer over the next six months until reaching Maine in the Fall. This hiker avoided the crowds by hiking through the winter, describing his journey as highly challenging, with nearly impassable snow for much of the trip. Grateful to have the snow behind him, he aimed to make good time for the remainder of his journey. We informed him of the forecasted snow flurries overnight, though nothing significant was expected. He thanked us and briskly continued on his way.

Our initial plan was to stay at Rausch Gap Shelter for the evening, but finding it occupied by other hikers, we opted to tent camp along Rausch Creek instead. While welcome to join the group at the shelter, we prefer carrying our tents and tenting out, a practice we maintain even when shelters are available. Mice can be a nuisance in shelters, chewing through backpacks for food, which is unsettling while trying to sleep. Also, the potential for snoring among ourselves could disrupt sleep for others. Packing foam earplugs is always prudent for such situations. Additionally, on cold and windy nights, tents provide better warmth by trapping body heat compared to the open sides of a shelter. Despite these considerations, we found an ideal campsite with a fire pit near a stream and ample firewood nearby—a perfect setting.

---

[29]Wayne E. Gross, *Guide to The Appalachian Trail in Pennsylvania* (Cogan Station, PA: Keystone Trails Association, 1998), 18, 121.

We went through our usual routine to set up camp. We first set up our tents in case an unexpected rain shower hit us. Nothing is worse than setting up a tent in the rain; you want to get the tent set up and eliminate that risk. Picking the location to pitch your tent is an interesting process. You are looking for a relatively flat and clear spot, not too far from others but not too close, which goes back to that snoring issue I mentioned earlier. You don't want to be rude and rush to the obvious best spot available, but someone has to use it, and if no one else casually occupies the space, you will.

You then do a quick survey of the tree limbs overhead to avoid pitching your tent in a spot that could be the final resting place for a rotting tree limb. At this point, no one has yet started to pitch their tent. Everyone is standing in the general vicinity of where they think their spot will be, and without any words spoken, you can sense that everyone is OK with the sleeping arrangements, and then they begin setting up their tents. I clear out any larger rocks or branches and then survey the slope of the land. You want to pitch your tent so that your head is on the high end. Otherwise, you will slide into your tent vestibule during the night. I say this from firsthand experience.

Once the tents are pitched, everyone begins gathering firewood. There is also a system for gathering firewood, but no one is aware that there is anything systematic to it; it just happens. You all disburse into different parts of the forest, looking for dry branches lying on the ground. You grab several large branches and then drag them back to the fire pit. Ideally, these branches have a two-inch or so diameter main stem used once the fire is established. Several one-inch branches get the fire to the point of putting larger branches on, and then a bunch of twigs will be used as kindling to start the fire.

At some point, one or two of you will begin breaking up the branches and sorting them by size while the others will

Spring Surprise

continue to gather wood. The smaller branches are broken by hand, and the larger branches are wedged in the "Y" of a tree and pushed on until they snap. Those continuing to gather wood are now focusing on well-dried two- to three-inch logs and probably won't see the fire for another hour or two. You might occasionally hear "Nice log" and then "Thanks" as the process continues. One of those breaking up the logs begins to make the fire.

There is no conversation about who will start the fire; it just happens. We all carry fire starters of some type, with my preference being a few chunks of wax-impregnated sawdust. Gathering wood and starting the fire takes about 20 minutes, and then you hear, "Nice fire," and then, "Thanks."

At this point, I hang a clothesline to air out my sweaty hiking clothes and change into my rain pants and jacket, which serve as my camp clothes. Depending on the air temperature, I may rinse off in the stream that we camped next to. Once I freshen up, I grab my food bag, stove, water bottles, and sitting pad and head to the campfire to cook, eat, and relax.

This night was a typical one around the campfire, enjoying the burning wood we had collected, and then we headed to our tents for the night. At this point, the forecasted snow flurries had not yet appeared. I slept soundly and got the typical ten hours plus of sleep that I usually get when on the trail. I woke to that same eerie stillness that I woke to on my Pinchot Trail hike. As I poked my head out of the tent, I couldn't believe that the forecasted "snow flurries" were at least six inches of snow, and it was still snowing. We ate our breakfast, standing around where the fire had burned the night before, packed up our tents, and then hit the trail.

We were all giddy at this point, like schoolboys who had played hooky. The scenery was fresh, brilliantly white, and magical. It was a little challenging following the snow-covered trail, and you had to take your time because your foot could hit a slippery rock covered by the snow.

I was wearing my knee-height gators, which turned my hiking boots into snow boots and kept the bottom of my pants from getting wet. I started wearing gators after my first few hikes and now wear them on every hike, no matter the conditions. None of my hiking buddies wear them regularly, and few other hikers I encounter wear gators. You could say that my preference for always wearing gators is unique. Wearing gators goes hand in hand with my refusal to carry an extra, clean pair of hiking pants in my backpack. Instead, I wear gators, which keep my only pair of pants clean from the dirt and mud on the trail. Gators also give me extra protection when walking through briars and stickers, and (now I know) turn my hiking boots into snow boots.

We crossed a bridge over Rausch Creek and then came to a sign that marked the location of the Village of Rausch Gap. Life must have been hard for them, but they had a beautiful setting for their little village. The trail had a 500-foot descent off Sharp Mountain, went through the Swatara State Park, and then crossed over Swatara Creek via an old iron bridge. It was a peaceful scene as we looked back on the snow-covered iron bridge with large snowflakes still falling from the sky. By this point, the snow had accumulated to about eight inches.

As is usually the case on the AT, a descent to a creek usually means climbing back up the next mountain. We then climbed 800 feet to the top of Blue Mountain and followed the ridge to William Penn Shelter, where we would spend the next night.

The William Penn Shelter had a loft, which meant the roof itself protected us from the wind. So, we laid out our air mattresses and sleeping bags in the loft and then headed out to gather firewood. The fallen snow made it a challenge to find firewood, but we were determined to gather enough wood for a fire. It was cold and breezy, so we built a substantial fire that warmed us up nicely despite the chill in the air.

We had our dinner, enjoyed the warmth of the fire, and then headed to the loft to sleep. It was much colder sleeping in the loft than expected. Even though we were sheltered by being in the loft, the wind under the loft floor chilled us from below. Regardless, the surprise of waking to the beauty of a snow-covered wilderness, creating fresh prints on the forest floor, and acting like kids again playing in the snow made up for the frigid night we spent in the loft.

I am reminded of another spring surprise that happened over 2000 years ago. Jesus was crucified on the cross because of his claim that he was the son of God. He was placed in a tomb and rose from the dead three days later on what we now know as Easter Sunday. When his disciples went to the tomb on Sunday morning, it was empty, and they assumed someone had stolen his body.

John 20:19-20 (NLT) tells us about the Disciple's Spring surprise: "That Sunday evening the disciples were meeting behind locked doors because they were afraid of the Jewish leaders. Suddenly, Jesus was standing there among them! 'Peace be with you,' he said. As he spoke, he showed them the wounds on his hands and his side. They were filled with joy when they saw the Lord!" Easter was the greatest spring surprise ever!

Jesus' death and resurrection are essential to all of humanity. Humans are sinful by nature and have no way to pay the penalty for our sins. Jesus, as God's son, is perfect and the only suitable substitute for our sins. By dying on the cross, Jesus took the punishment for our sins. The penalty has been paid. Then, by rising from the dead, Jesus showed that he had power over death and offered us the same benefit.

When you believe that Jesus died on the cross and rose from the dead and accept God's forgiveness, he will give you the gift of eternal life. Though your body dies, your spirit will live with him for eternity. This future is the final destination for those on the path of life.

On Sunday, we had a five-mile hike that continued on the ridge of Blue Mountain to our vehicle, which was parked on Route 501. Once we were back on the highway heading home, we could see that the eight-inch snowfall was isolated from the mountainous area we were hiking. This spring surprise made for one of my most memorable hikes ever. Without a doubt, some of life's best experiences happen when you least expect them!

Chapter Seventeen
LIGHTEN YOUR LOAD

The plan was for the five of us to do a 26-mile loop in The Great Smoky Mountains National Park. It would be me, Denny, Mark, Tom, and Trent. We had all hiked together in the past, and the anticipation for this one was high as the date approached. Schedules had been accommodated, hiking permits completed, and food purchases made. It was Tuesday, and we were leaving for the Smoky Mountains on Thursday. A look at the extended forecast stopped us dead in our tracks. A storm was on its way to Tennessee, and it would be a four-day hike with a nearly 100% chance of rain. I am okay with the thought of a day or two of less-than-perfect weather, but to hike in the rain for an entire trip was not something that any of us wanted to risk.

With an eye on the weather reports and my hands on my trail maps, I chose a 29-mile hike on the Loyalsock Trail in Pennsylvania. This route would be 530 miles north of the Smoky Mountains, far from that nasty forecast. It felt good to pivot so quickly, knowing that any solid plan needs to be flexible. The Loyalsock Trail is 59 miles long, and we would hike the lower half of the trail with the help of a vehicle shuttle. We drove two vehicles to a point that was just about the midpoint on Dry Run Road and parked one of them. Then, we all piled into the remaining vehicle and drove it to the starting point on Route 87. From there, we would backpack to the vehicle parked on Dry Run Road.

This route was a trail I had hiked before, and it was an excellent opportunity to try out my new hammock. The hammock purchase was part of my ever-present goal of decreasing my pack weight. The hammock had two components: a lightweight hammock with mosquito netting and a tarp suspended over the hammock to protect it from the elements. This system was 20 ounces lighter than my tent and eliminated the need to carry a 20-ounce air mattress. This option saved me from carrying over two pounds and was a great addition to my inventory of backpacking equipment.

There is a natural progression in accumulating an inventory of backpacking equipment and clothing. Borrowing equipment is an essential first step in the process. Who has an extra grand or two to buy everything you need to do a hike, only to discover that you don't enjoy the body odor and blisters from spending three days in the woods? Once you decide that this is something you want to do, you begin putting the puzzle pieces together. Your goal is to depend less and less on others for the missing pieces. Camp stoves and water purification systems are both examples of items that you can borrow and, at the same time, help your fellow hikers. "Hey, I don't have a stove yet. Can I use yours? Sure, you carry it, and we can both use it." See what I mean? At some point, the puzzle is complete. You now have everything you need to spend three days in the woods without borrowing anything.

During your initial purchase of equipment, you buy the best you can afford, but your decisions are full of compromises. For example, most hikers wear two pairs of socks when hiking. The first pair is called liner socks, which are very thin, lightweight socks. The second pair is the actual hiking sock, which is heavier. Your sweat is trapped between the two pairs of socks, which keeps your feet drier and less prone to blisters. Also, wearing two pairs of socks absorbs the friction you create when hiking, and this also reduces blisters. My compromise was to forego the official six-dollar pair of liner socks and use a pair of nylon dress socks instead.

Another process involves eliminating some items altogether. A mental note of things you carried for 30 miles on your back, which returned home unused, should be the first items to go. The hand axe and six-inch saw are examples of items you leave at home once you see how easy it is to break logs in the "Y" of a tree. All you need to do is wedge a log in the "Y" of a tree and push on it until it snaps.

An exception to the "leave it at home" rule is things that you carry for safety purposes. My main source for water purification is a ultraviolet light water purifier, which operates on lithium batteries and uses ultraviolet light to purify water. I carry backup batteries, which I have used, but I also pack iodine tablets if the ultraviolet light water purifier fails. I have never resorted to using the iodine tablets, but I still carry them just in case. Another example is taking two small plastic bags if I step into the water and totally soak my hiking boots. I plan to put dry socks on and then put the plastic bags over the dry socks to keep them from absorbing the water in the boots. I have never used these plastic bags, but I continue to carry them, just in case. If this scenario ever happens, I calculate that the low weight of the plastic bags is worth the comfort I will enjoy from dry socks.

Then, you start to decrease the quantities of what you carry. You decide that a partial roll of toilet paper is all you need and that a clean pair of underwear every other day is fine. You also realize that some things in your pack can serve two purposes. Your clothes sack is a good substitute for a pillow, and the mini-pillow can now stay at home. Your rain gear can serve as evening camp clothes while your hiking clothes are hanging out to dry, and your evening camp clothes can be eliminated.

Lastly, you start to upgrade what you have. Sure, I have six extra bucks and can now afford actual liner socks instead of putting holes in my dress socks. Upgrades are very well-researched and contemplated. It is no longer a matter of wanting what you can afford; you now want the best available. Regarding backpacking gear, "the best" is synonymous with "the lightest." There is an inverse relationship between an item's weight and its cost. The lighter something is, the more costly it is. Yes, with backpacking gear, you get less for more! There are, of course, other considerations such as durability, efficiency, and design, so the lightweight model with the most durable and efficient design wins.

You are now purchasing items you can no longer afford. I decided to sell my Ithaca lever-action .22-caliber rifle to upgrade some of my backpacking equipment. That I sold the rifle to a fellow backpacker somehow softened the blow. You know you are becoming a backpacking equipment junkie when you start to sell family heirlooms to support your habit.

At about the same time, I started purchasing backpacking equipment so my wife could join me. There was now a two-dimensional aspect to my purchases. I needed a matching pair of sleeping bags so they could be joined together at the zippers to

Lighten Your Load

make one large sleeping bag for us. However, one of the stand-alone bags could now be used as my summer bag when hiking without Cindy. I had arrived. I now had enough gear to equip myself and lend it to others who still needed their gear. This extra equipment enabled me to allow newbies to share in my passion. This included friends, co-workers, and family members.

For my first hike with Dave on the Loyalsock Trail, I was quite pleased that I was able to reduce my pack weight to 42 pounds. Thirteen years and many dollars later, with the help of this new hammock system, my pack weight was down to 27 pounds. Carrying less weight makes for a more enjoyable hike, especially as you age.

Just as carrying too much weight in your pack on a hike will slow you down, sin in your life will spiritually slow you down. Hebrews 12:1-2 (NLT) says, "...let us strip off every weight that slows us down, especially the sin that so easily trips us up." We sin when we do something God does not want us to do or don't do something God has for us to do. Another way to describe sin is that it is "missing the mark." The picture is of a target; if the shooter does not hit the target, they are missing the mark. You are not alone in your susceptibility to sin or missing the mark. Sin becomes an obstacle between us and God and slows our spiritual growth. Sin is a common problem for all of humanity. Romans 3:23 (NLT) says, "For everyone has sinned; we all fall short of God's glorious standard." We all share a common problem, sin, but the good news is that we all have access to a common solution.

When you believe that Jesus died on the cross and rose from the dead and accept God's gift of forgiveness, the

Holy Spirit comes to live in you. The Holy Spirit lives within you and is there to help you grow in your faith. When we sin, it is pointed out to us by the Holy Spirit, and we are compelled to change. If we don't change, the Holy Spirit will continue to remind us of the change we need to make. There is a battle between what your body wants and what the Holy Spirit asks you to do. It is this battle that slows us down in our spiritual growth.

The good news is that we no longer have to be controlled by our sinful nature. In Romans 6:14 (NLT), Paul tells us, "Sin is no longer your master...". Now that the Holy Spirit is living within you, he can change your desires and help you overcome the sin that controls you.

There are some biblical and practical things you can do to move beyond the sin that is slowing you down. James 4:7 (NLT) says; "Submit yourselves, then, to God. Resist the devil, and he will flee from you." By submitting to God, through prayer and reading the Bible, you are filling yourself with more of God so there is less room for the sin to thrive. By resisting the devil, you are recognizing the source of the temptation and not yielding to that temptation. Each time you resist the temptation you are establishing better habits and distancing yourself from your enemy the devil. On the practical end, there may be a venue or person that contributes to your pattern of sin. You may have to avoid certain situations or people that are a gateway to the sin that you are yielding to.

What I just described are behaviors that describe "how" God can help you break a pattern of sin. It is also valuable to consider "why" you should change your behavior. As a parent, I learned the value of letting my kids know why I am asking them to behave in a certain way. God is our heavenly father and as his children, the Bible details many benefits of following his instructions. First, there is a freedom and joy that comes with submitting to God. Imagine being free from the cycle of sin that was sidetracking you to the point that the sin becomes a distant memory.[30] This is not to say that you will attain a position where you are no longer tempted or sinless, we will always be in the process of being transformed and being made more like Jesus. What I am presenting is not being trapped or slowed down by one sin that keeps you from moving forward. There is an amazing joy that comes from being free from this type of sin.

A second reason why you should change your behavior is so that you can have a purer connection and relationship with God. Instead of spending your prayer time confessing and repenting of a sin addiction that you have, you can spend your prayer time fellowshipping with God.

A third benefit of changing your behavior are the promised blessings attached to obeying God. Psalm 1:1-3 (NLT) says; "Oh, the joys of those who do not follow the advice of the wicked, or stand around with sinners, or join in with mockers. But they delight in the law of the Lord, meditating on it day and night. They are like trees planted along the riverbank, bearing fruit

---

[30]John Eldredge, The Utter Relief of Holiness (New York, NY: Hachette Book Group, 2013), 43.

each season. Their leaves never wither, and they prosper in all they do."

Being free from the sin that has you captive needs to be a priority in your walk with God. If you hit an impasse and are not able to see a victory, you should seek out additional counseling or treatment from a qualified faith-based counselor. I would also recommend John Eldredge's book, The Utter Relief of Holiness as an additional resource. The benefits of breaking free from a sin that we are bound to are very compelling. The Holy Spirit within you and your willingness to submit to God will keep you on the path of life as you are enjoying those benefits.

Our plan for a backpacking trip in the Smoky Mountains was put on the back burner, and we began a 29-mile hike on the Loyalsock Trail. We hiked eight miles on Thursday, which included a 1,235-foot climb as soon as we hit the trail. The climb was a challenge, and I kept reminding myself how much harder it was 13 years earlier when I did it with Dave. For that hike, I had 42 pounds on my back instead of the new pack weight of 27 pounds. We soaked in the view at Smiths Knob Vista and then descended to camp at Painters Run.

 We hiked six miles on Friday and then camped at the junction of the two branches of Hessler Run. On Saturday, we hiked 11 miles through a historical area once home to several hotels during the logging boom, past Spring Window with a view of Angel Falls, and then camped at Kettle Creek. This left us with a four-mile hike on Sunday, which was an "easy out" to get us home early. It rained most of the morning on Sunday and made us all thankful that we didn't have a solid four days of rain.

Lighten Your Load

As I looked over the photos of this hike, I was reminded of how much further away from the rest of the group I had to be to find the perfect distance between two trees to use my hammock. Another issue with the hammock is the "butt breeze" you get suspended between two trees. I would not advise using a hammock in cooler temperatures. I had a great night's sleep in the hammock, but some complained of lower back pain because of the lack of support. As with many things in life, there is no perfect solution, and that's why having more options created by having a bigger backpacking equipment inventory is always better!

Chapter Eighteen
WHY I BACKPACK

Mark floated the idea several times, but I knew what was involved with a trip like this and was not interested. I knew he was getting serious when he sent me an email attachment describing a nine-day trip to Tanzania to climb Mount Kilimanjaro to its summit at 19,345 feet. The trip included five nights at base camps to prepare everyone's bodies for the elevation changes as the group of hikers and sherpas made their way up the face of the dormant volcano. For now, Mark's request was simple: he wanted to do a backpacking trip to a higher elevation to see how his body responded to the higher altitudes.

Being able to handle higher altitudes is more complex than spending extra time in the gym to condition your body; each person handles higher altitudes differently. For some, the lower oxygen at a higher altitude will make them short of breath and winded; for others, the result could be altitude sickness accompanied by headache, confusion, lack of coordination, and vomiting.[31] Mark wanted to see how his body would react. I was game to be part of a higher elevation hike, but I wasn't interested in signing up for the climb up Mount Kilimanjaro.

The conversation about Mount Kilimanjaro began in June. By December, Tom, Mark, and I had tentative plans to do several hikes in the Grand Teton National Park in Wyoming. We were now waiting for January when the National Parks Service would issue a fresh batch of backcountry permits. I logged onto the park website as soon as they were made available and secured my first choice. With the permits in hand, we made our flight reservations to fly into Jackson Hole on a Thursday in late August and return from Jackson Hole the following Wednesday.

I purchased the largest duffel bag on wheels that the airlines would allow without added fees. I prepacked it to ensure it held all my backpacking equipment without exceeding the 50-pound limit. This included my bear canister but did not include lithium batteries, stove fuel, and bear spray, which you cannot transport on a flight. These items would have to be purchased once we arrived in Jackson Hole.

We scheduled the earliest flight possible because we wanted to hike on our first day in the park. Once we landed, there was a lot to accomplish. We picked up our rental SUV, went to an outfitter in Jackson Hole to get our lithium batteries, stove fuel, and bear spray, and then headed to the Lupine Meadows Trail Head, where we parked the SUV.

---

[31] Amy Rost, *Survival Wisdom & Know-How* (New York, NY: Black Dog and Leventhal Publishers, 2007), 763.

This would be an eight-mile roundtrip hike to Delta Lake that we did with just our daypacks on. Delta Lake's allure was that it was not a trail highlighted by the Park Service, and I learned about this "secret spot" through a hiker's post on their website. You follow the signs and trails towards Surprise & Amphitheater Lakes from Lupine Meadows. While following the trail through an open meadow, you will view Bradley Lake below. There will be an intersection of Garnet Canyon Trail and Amphitheater Lake Trail, where you should stay to the right on Amphitheater Lake Trail. You will leave the maintained trail on the first switchback after this intersection. It is easy to miss if you are not looking for it, so keep an eye out for a footpath that leaves the maintained trail to the right.

Once we were on the unmarked path, rock cairns were placed where the footpath was not well defined. This unmaintained trail involved several rock scrambles and a final 500-foot climb to the lake. The glacial lake had a turquoise hue, surrounded by the snow-dusted Teton Mountains, with large pine trees boarding its shoreline. The lake's remoteness and breathtaking setting made it a perfect hike to start our trip.

The adrenaline of hiking to our first destination subsided, and on our way back to the SUV, wildflowers in the open meadows caught our attention. It was late August in the Tetons, and we saw many blooming throughout our trip.

Our next stop for the day was to set up a base camp at the Colter Bay Village and Campground. By our standards, this was luxury camping with running water, showers, and a picnic table. We set up our tents, which would stay for the next three nights as we took various day trips.

Our Friday hike was structured around Mark's request for a higher altitude one. Because we didn't know how our bodies would handle the higher altitude, we didn't want to risk making this part of a two-day or three-day hike if one of us got too sick to continue. At least on a day hike, if one of us could not move forward, we could return to our vehicle. It took a bit of research and consideration to find a higher altitude climb day hike that was within our hiking capabilities. We chose the 14-mile roundtrip hike to Table Mountain, which has an elevation of 11,106 feet.

We drove two hours to the Teton Canyon Trailhead which sits at 6,800 feet. The summit has two approaches: a steep and challenging four-mile climb and an easier seven-mile climb. We took the easier seven-mile climb, which followed the North Teton Trail and paralleled North Teton Creek. The trail went through several flower-covered meadows, and parts of it were lined with aspen trees. For the last mile and a half, we were above the tree line and treated to an excellent view of the upcoming mountain range.

At this point, we were a mile and a half from the summit and at 9,900 feet elevation. We checked in with each other and were all doing fine, except for being a little out of breath. Once we were about three-quarters of a mile from the summit, and at 10,500 feet, we felt sluggish and had trouble catching our breath.

At about this time, a family with two young children briskly walked past us, heading in the other direction on the trail. They must have been locals accustomed to the higher elevation because they appeared unaffected by it.

From then on, we could only walk about 40 yards before feeling exhausted. We would stop and break for a few minutes and then continue our slow ascent, 40 yards at a time until we reached the summit. The last 80 yards was a fairly steep rock scramble. Once on the summit, we had a panoramic view of the Teton Range with the 13,775-foot Grand Teton peak immediately in front of us. I quickly soaked it all in and then sat down on the summit, feeling like I was going to vomit.

I forced myself to hold it in because several bystanders were there, and I didn't want to gross them out.

After a few minutes, my stomach settled down, and I could stand up and enjoy the view. As is typically the case, there was a howling wind as we stood on the summit. I've experienced this several times over my years of backpacking, and it never ceases to amaze me how the environment changes once you reach a summit. There were endless mountain ranges in every direction you looked, and it was an inspiring sight. We spent ten minutes on the summit and then headed back down.

My nausea subsided, but I started to develop a headache. We were about a quarter mile from the summit when I got a bad cramp in my abdomen. I have experienced these before when backpacking, and I knew the best way to treat them was to lie down on my back and relax. At this point, Mark and Tom were freaking out, thinking I was having a heart attack or something. I assured them I was okay, rested a little, drank water, and took a few aspirin.

It was obvious to me that my body did not handle changes in altitude well, and I am okay with that. When you ask backpackers, hikers, or mountain climbers why they do what they do, many frequently respond that they enjoy the physical challenge of pushing their bodies beyond what they want to do. I appreciate what they say and enjoy the physical challenge backpacking offers. However, the physical challenge is not the main reason I backpack and probably why I am not enthused about joining Mark on his Mount Kilimanjaro trip.

Times like being on Table Top Mountain bring me to the point of asking, why am I putting myself through this? Why do I backpack? There are definitely some things about backpacking that keep me coming back despite some of the physical challenges. I enjoy planning a safe and enjoyable trip and seeing it go according to plan. I also like being able to pivot and change the plan when the trip goes sideways so that I can safely finish the hike.

I love experiencing God's creation on the trail. Whether encountering wildlife, gazing at a remote glacial lake, feeling the mist of water at the base of a waterfall, or seeing wildflowers in a mountain meadow, I am reminded that this was all created by an extraordinary God for our enjoyment. Backpacking is an opportunity to disconnect from the world's comforts and reconnect with God.

I am thrilled by cresting a mountain's summit to a far-reaching view and even more so if the mountain is tall enough to be accompanied by a howling wind. I am comforted by the rhythm you sink into through the daily routine of walking, eating, and sleeping, and I find it a welcome relief from the complexities of everyday life. I find backpacking to be a therapeutic experience of solitude. It allows me to process life's challenges and reflect on my thoughts without distraction.

Building relationships with strangers, friends, coworkers, or family enriches my backpacking experiences. While solo hikes hold their own value, shared hikes often surpass solitude. Arriving at a mountain stream campsite is a highlight of many hikes. Setting up camp, collecting firewood, changing into dry clothes, and relaxing by the firepit are satisfying rituals.

However, backpacking also has its drawbacks. Knee pain persists despite trekking poles, reduced pack weight, and conditioning, especially on steep descents. Sore, swollen feet, and occasional lost toenails from challenging hikes are common. Enduring days of dirt and sweat discomforts me; rinsing in mountain streams helps, but nothing beats a hot shower at home.

Summer hiking brings bugs, heat, humidity, and scarce water. I recall mosquito-filled nights huddled over smoky firepits for relief. While rain gear offers protection, hiking in the rain still means soaking in sweat trapped by waterproofed rain gear.

Bathroom breaks in the woods, especially at night, remain inconvenient. Exiting a cozy sleeping bag and struggling with fogged eyeglasses and sometimes rain gear is routine but necessary. Lastly, there's no graceful way to manage nature's call in the woods—digging a pit, squatting beside a log, using wipes, then covering the pit is never dignified, yet essential.

Despite these challenges, the rewards of backpacking—the physical, emotional, and spiritual growth, the beauty of nature, and the camaraderie of fellow hikers—keep me returning to the trail. These are why I continue to backpack despite the hardships that sometimes come with it.

There is a paradox for me when it comes to backpacking. Initially, there is the planning stage for each hike, and the anticipation builds as the hike date approaches. The day arrives, and you are on the trail. Returning to the trail feels great; you look forward to the joys and challenges ahead.

As the miles grind on, you start to calculate how many miles you have until you can take a lunch break and get some relief from the weight of the pack. You feel refreshed from your lunch break, but now start calculating the miles until you can set up camp in the evening. On days two and three, you begin to slip into the rhythm of being on the trail, but in the back of your mind, you are counting down the remaining miles before you are in your SUV heading back home. It is a paradox. Why am I so anxious for something to end that I was looking forward to doing so much?

I am now in my SUV, heading home. I drive along the base of the mountain that I just hiked, and it takes me ten minutes to drive past an area that took me a whole day to hike on foot. We stop at a diner for a post-hike meal, and while the oatmeal eaten out of a plastic bag hit the spot just two hours earlier, it does not compare to the crispy bacon, cheese omelet, and home fries I am now enjoying. Once I arrive home, I kiss Cindy quickly, knowing I will hug her once showered. I hang my tent and sleeping bag outside to dry, then clean and put away the rest of my backpacking equipment. I then get a hot shower, which feels amazing as the salty, dried sweat rinses off my body. After the shower, I head to the kitchen, where Cindy has a cup of coffee waiting for me. We have an extended hug, sit down to enjoy a cup of coffee together, and share how our last few days went.

For me, backpacking is an opportunity to reboot and refocus on what is essential in life. Yes, you experience some awesome things on each trip, but there are an equal number of challenges. Spending a few days in the woods helps me remember how blessed I am and helps me appreciate the comforts of home. It is easy to take life for granted and forget how good a prepared meal, hot shower, and long hug can feel. I backpack because it adjusts my perspective and helps me fully appreciate my life.

We hiked the seven miles from Table Top Mountain back to the trailhead, and my headache was gone when I got in the SUV. We drove back two hours to Colter Bay Village & Campground, stopping at Bubba's Bar-B-Que. We knew today's hike would be challenging, so we built a "recovery day" into our schedule for Saturday.

For our recovery day, we drove one hour north to Yellowstone National Park and did the things most tourists do. We visited the most famous geyser, Old Faithful, took photos of each other standing next to a buffalo, drove to a vista overlooking the Yellowstone River, and toured a hot spring. Yellowstone National Park contains many amazing natural wonders but many more people than I am used to seeing in the wilderness.

Why I Backpack

By Saturday evening, dusk was falling, and we were back in Teton National Park, driving around looking for an elk herd. We knew we found an elk herd when several other cars pulled onto the road's shoulder. We were taking photos of the elk when I got a call from Cindy. Our cell connection was not the best, but I got the message that my mom had passed away. My mom was 95 years old and in failing health. It was news that I had not expected, and she was on my mind for much of the remaining trip.

We packed up our base camp Sunday morning and prepared for our three-day backcountry hike. We first stopped at the Ranger Station to register and pick up the backcountry permits we had reserved earlier in the year and then headed to the Granite Canyon Trailhead, where we parked the SUV. The permits enabled us to hike the 25-mile Granite Canyon / Death Canyon Loop. Sunday would be a 9-mile hike on Granite Canyon Trail and Teton Crest Trail to Marion Lake, where we would camp. Monday would be a 7-mile hike on the Teton Crest Trail and then the Death Canyon Trail. We would be camping in Death Canyon. Tuesday would be a 9-mile hike on Death Canyon Trail, Valley Trail, and then Granite Canyon Trail back to the SUV.

The Sunday hike on Granite Canyon Trail was through flower-filled meadows. It followed the crystal-clear Granite Creek, which had several beautiful waterfalls. It was fairly easy hiking, and my thoughts were filled with memories of my mom.

My dad fell off the roof of a building that he was inspecting when he was just 46 years old and died as a result of the fall. I was the youngest of four children at the age of ten. My mom put the four of us through college, and for several years, it was just my mom and me still at home.

Backpacking & the Path of Life

I remember how she would be up early on Saturday mornings to clean the house because she was working a full-time job during the week. She would have something baking in the oven, and I'm not sure if that lured me out of bed or if the vacuum cleaner's noise did.

She knew how much I enjoyed the outdoors, and when I was a junior in high school, we flew west to Colorado where we rented a car, bought camping equipment, and toured the state's wilderness areas. One of the places we visited was Pike's Peak, which has an elevation of 14,115 feet. The altitude gave us both headaches, but my mom's headache brought her to tears, and we had to take a break at the summit for her to recover.

My thoughts drifted in and out like this for the next two days, and being on the trail helped me process the fact that she was gone and how much I was going to miss her. More than anything, I was comforted by Jesus' words in John 11:25 (NLT) when he said, "I am the resurrection and the life. Anyone who believes in me will live, even after dying. Everyone who lives in me and believes in me will never ever die."

Because of the seven years I served on a church staff, I have been to more funerals than the average person. There is a distinct difference between attending the funeral of someone who had a relationship with Jesus and attending the funeral of someone who did not. The scriptures may have been similar, but there is an unmistakable joy for those who know their loved ones are now in heaven.

I knew without a doubt that my mom had a relationship with God and that I would see her again in heaven.

Why I Backpack

I knew she was on the path of life and now enjoying her final destination. This truth comforted me and gave me hope as I processed how much I would miss her.

The climb throughout the day was gradual, going from 6,500 feet at the trailhead to 9,250 feet at Marion Lake. The wind picked up as we arrived at Marion Lake, and we helped each other set up our tents. The wind made staking a tent more challenging than usual. We then had dinner on a vista overlooking Marion Lake and the ravine we had just hiked.

As we were sitting there, a park ranger joined us on the vista. He explained that he traveled to the remote backcountry campsite to warn hikers of an approaching storm. He said the temperatures would drop below freezing, and severe winds would accompany snow or freezing rain. He then commended us on our selection of places to have dinner and told us that we might see a mountain lion that makes its home in the rocks on the peak across from our vista. We kept an eye out for the mountain lion but never saw it. It was reassuring to know that the park service was watching out for hikers in the backcountry, and it shows the value of the backcountry permit system.

I put a few extra tent stakes in the ground to secure my tent and headed in for the night. The wind was extremely strong throughout the night, and I woke several times to the sound and sight of my tent sides being tested.

On Monday morning, we woke to the sound of sleet and packed up our campsite. You never want to pack a wet tent, but we had no choice. For one thing, it meant we would be pitching wet tents later that evening, but it also meant we had to carry the extra water weight contained in wet tents. A coating of sleet covered the trail as we exited the Marion Lake area and headed toward Death Canyon. We were in full rain gear with the crunching of sleet underfoot and the sound of sleet hitting the leaves and ground. It was a cold, breezy, sleety, rainy, and overall miserable day to hike.

We were on the edge of the forest when we spotted a bull moose step out of the forest and into the meadow. All three of us instantly stopped and pulled out our cameras. Very soon, a second bull moose popped out of the forest, and both were heading in our direction. They were unbothered by our presence and foraged on some tree leaves in the meadow, passing by at most 20 yards from where we stood. It was captivating to witness the moose in their natural environment doing what they do without concern about us standing there; this experience made the miserable day of hiking worth it!

Our hike from Marion Lake to our campsite in Death Canyon was only seven miles, and we made it there early in the afternoon. There was a brief let-up in the rain, and we quickly set up our wet tents before it started to rain again. Nothing was left to do but sink into our sleeping bags and call it a day.

Mark, Tom, and I could hear each other from our tents, and I learned from Tom that his wet tent had gotten his sleeping bag wet while it was in his backpack. Tom was chilled and had to wear all his clothes to get warm. Mark was chilled and put his foil emergency blanket over his sleeping bag to help him warm up, but it appeared that the emergency blanket was trapping in his body moisture and dampening the outside of his sleeping bag. I encouraged Mark to wear more clothes and stop using the emergency blanket.

It was about nine o'clock Monday evening when I woke and heard no more rain. I got out of my tent and made myself dinner. Not hearing any noise from Tom or Mark's tents, I returned to my tent and slept for the rest of the night. I had over 14 hours of sleep that night but stayed dry and felt refreshed when I finally got up. Tom later told me that he was chilled most of the night and had the worst and coldest night's

Why I Backpack

sleep ever. As we were packing up our campsite, there was a distant rumble and the sound of crashing rocks from a rock slide. None of us had heard this before, and we were glad it wasn't closer than it sounded.

Tuesday was the last day of our hike, and it would take us the rest of the way through Death Canyon and then back to our SUV. It was a beautiful day with spectacular scenery, including several large waterfalls full from the previous day's rain. When we returned to the trailhead, we dried our tents, sleeping bags, and clothes in preparation for our flight home the next day. We had dinner at Pinky G's Pizzeria and then opted to stay at a hotel Tuesday night so we could get cleaned up before our trip home.

This trip had a great amount of variety. It included both the things I enjoy about backpacking and the things that challenge me: the day hike to the remote Delta Lake, the meadows filled with wildflowers, the day hike to the summit at Table Top Mountain with its view of the Grand Teton peak, my altitude sickness at Table Top Mountain, the day trip to Yellowstone to see its many natural wonders, the opportunity to process my mom's passing on my way to Marion Lake, the windy night spent at Marion Lake, the cold sleeting hike in Death Canyon, the encounter with the two moose in Death Canyon, the wet and cold night in Death Canyon, and the chance to spend a week in the wilderness with two of my backpacking buddies.

Every backpacking trip has its own list of blessings and challenges but I always return home with a greater gratitude for the life I have been given. Backpacking reboots my perspective and helps me fully appreciate my life. I wouldn't change a thing about the trip we had planned, and now I know that my body is not cut out for higher altitudes, but at the same time, I know that Mark's is. Mark, send me a pic of Mount Kilimanjaro once you arrive!

EPILOGUE

Experiencing backpacking has given me a different perspective and understanding of the scriptures as I read them.

Adam and Eve were created by God and placed in the Garden to enjoy all of His creation. I now have a greater appreciation for some of what they must have experienced. Moses was led to the wilderness, where he wandered around for 40 years. During that time, the Israelites lived in tents and ate the same food every day, and I imagine they fell into the rhythm of walking, eating, and sleeping. Moses also climbed a mountain to receive the Ten Commandments from God. Certainly, John the Baptist, who lived in the wilderness and off the land, would have excelled as an AT thru-hiker. Jesus spent much time in the wilderness, walked countless miles throughout his ministry, and climbed a mountain with Peter, James, and John, where they met Moses and Elijah.

The Bible is also full of symbolism that uses elements in nature to describe our journey through life. Mountains are portrayed as challenges or obstacles in life. Valleys are portrayed as places of sadness and despair. Streams are symbolic of the spiritual life we receive from God. The wilderness or desert is where we go to be tried and purified. Storms are symbolic of the trials we go through in life. Rocks symbolize the stability we find in God.

I hope that my backpacking stories will enhance your backpacking experience. I also hope that the scriptures I presented will ignite in you a desire to start or maintain your journey on the path of life. Below is a summary of the scriptures I used for you to reference in the future as you grow in your relationship with God. How would you respond to these challenges?

- Do I love the Lord with all my heart, soul, mind, and strength? (Matthew 22:37)
- Do I cast my anxiety on Jesus? (1 Peter 5:7)
- Do I have a mentor who challenges me, and am I a mentor to others? (Mark 3:14)
- Am I part of a church body, or am I trying to do life on my own? (Ecclesiastes 4:12)
- Do I know how to commit my plans to God? (Proverbs 16:3)
- Am I consumed by fear and worry? (Matthew 6:25-34)
- Have I learned to rejoice when I encounter problems and trials? (Romans 5:3-4)
- Do I thirst for God? (Psalms 42:1)
- Do I share with others the hope that I have in God? (1 Peter 3:15-16)
- Am I wearing all of God's armor so I can battle the enemy? (Ephesians 6:11-17)
- Are my eyes open to see God at work in my life? (1 Thessalonians 5:16-17)
- Is God's Word my guide in the darkness? (Psalm 119:105)
- Do I appreciate the vastness of God's creation? (Psalms 104:24-25)
- Have I entered the race to receive the heavenly prize? (Philippians 3:14)
- Am I praying daily and persistently? (Luke 11:9-10)
- Do I understand what Jesus' resurrection means for me? (John 20:19-20)
- Am I weighed down by any sin in my life? (Hebrews 12:1-2)
- Do I have the hope of eternal life? (John 11:25)

Epilogue

God knew what he was doing when he birthed this passion for backpacking in my heart. It suited me well, drew me closer to him, and allowed me to help others experience the same thing. I am so glad that I could share my backpacking experiences with you and my journey on the path of life!

Appendix One

BACKPACKING HANDOUT FOR NEWBIE

I am going to describe what you will wear and carry on the upcoming backpacking trip. I am providing most of the equipment that you will need but there will be some items that you have to supply as well. I caution you against overpacking. You will have to carry everything you pack and a heavier pack makes for a less enjoyable experience. The tendency is to pack more clothing and food then you need. Be very selective about what you pack. As you climb a mountain with a pack on your back every ounce makes a difference.

What should you wear on your feet?

A good pair of hiking shoes or boots is the most important item you will wear. Sneakers are not a good alternative. Work boots may be a good substitute as long as they don't weigh more than six pounds for the pair. If you buy a pair of boots just for this hike, make sure that you break them in before you use for hiking.

The norm is to wear two pair of socks. The first pair of socks is called a liner sock which is thin and made of synthetic material. A pair of nylon dress socks would make a good liner sock. The second pair of socks should be a heavier hiking sock. Wearing two pairs of socks will protect against getting blisters.

What type of clothing should you wear?

Avoid cotton clothing which absorbs moisture. It is best to wear pants and a long sleeve T-shirt made of synthetic material such as polyester. A lot of sports gear is made out of synthetic material and works well. I also suggest that you wear a baseball cap.

What extra clothing should you pack?

- Since you are only wearing a T-shirt when you are hiking, you should pack a jacket or fleece that you will put on when you stop hiking to protect you from getting chilled. You will also wear the jacket or fleece around camp in the evenings.
- An extra long sleeve T-shirt that you will wear in camp for the evening(s) and on your last day of hiking.
- An extra set of socks and undergarments for each day you will be hiking.
- Stocking cap and gloves to wear in camp for the evening.
- Water shoes or sandals to wear for stream crossings and in camp each evening.

Put all of your extra clothing in a plastic bag just big enough to hold your clothes.

What food should you pack?

You will need food that is high in calories, light to carry, and easy to prepare. You will not be cooking food over a fire. Instead, you will be boiling water that will be used to hydrate the food you are carrying. You will hydrate your food in a plastic bag and then eat the food directly out of the plastic bag. I am going to describe the food I will be bringing and then you can either do the same or else bring what you think will best satisfy you.

Each Breakfast
- Instant oatmeal with nuts and raisins in zip-lock bag.
- Bagel and a small quantity of peanut butter.
- Coffee in zip-lock bag.

Each Lunch
- Trail mix.
- 3 Energy bars.

Each Dinner
- Freeze dried meal.
- Dessert such as Rice Crispy Treat.

Put all of your food in a gallon zip-lock baggie.

What toiletries should you pack?

- Toothbrush and small tube of toothpaste.
- Small roll of toilet paper, handy-wipes.
- Small container of bio-degradable soap.
- Cloth hankie for each day.
- Preferred pain killer such as aspirin.

Put all of your toiletries in a gallon zip-lock baggie.

What other items should you pack?

- Plastic mug for coffee or tea if you drink.
- Spoon, matches, headlamp.
- Rope for clothes line (12' of ¼" poly rope).

Put all of your other items in a gallon zip-lock baggie.

What will I provide that you will carry?

- Backpack & backpack cover.
- Tent.
- Sleeping Bag.
- Air mattress.
- Sitting pad.
- Two one-liter water bottles.
- Trekking poles.
- Rainsuit (this should also go in your clothes bag).

What will I provide for you to use that I will carry?

- Stove to boil water & water purifier.
- Filter to make coffee.
- Fire starters.
- Map.
- First aid kit which includes nail clippers, first aid cream, and mole skin.

Also pack ...

You should also pack a daypack with clean clothes for the ride home. We will be stopping at a restaurant for a post hike meal and you (and others) will appreciate having fresh clothes on. Here is my end of hike daypack list ...

- Hair brush & deodorant.
- Fresh socks and under garments.
- Jeans, shirt, and sneakers.
- Plastic trash bag to hold dirty hike clothes.

Appendix Two
BACKPACK PACKING LIST

List for a three-day and two-night Northeast US Autumn Hike

Backpack – Main

- Sleeping Bag
- Tent with stakes
- Inflatable sleeping pad
- Gas stove and fuel

Food Sack

- Spoon
- Plastic coffee mug with coffee filter
- Coffee
- Instant oatmeal-2
- Bagles-2
- Peanut butter
- Dehydrated meals-2
- Dessert bars-2
- Energy bars-4

Clothes Sack

- Plastic bags in case boots get wet-2
- Plastic bag for wash
- Cloth hankies-2
- Liner socks-2

- Socks-2
- Undergarments-2
- Knit cap
- Poly long T-shirt
- Rain jacket and pants

Misc. Hardware in Large Zip Lock Bag
- Rope for clothes line
- Rope & carabineer to hang food
- Fire starters & matches
- Headlamp
- Extra batteries for lamp and water purifier

Toiletries Large Zip Lock Bag
- Tooth paste & tooth brush
- Liquid soap
- Toilet paper
- Hand wipes-6

Medical Large Zip Lock Bag
- Asprin-9
- Mole skin
- First-aid cream
- Nail clippers, file, needle, scissors, knife
- Matches
- Iodine tables

Backpack – Lid

- Energy bars-2
- Trail Mix
- Water purifier
- Smartphone and accessories

- Map & mechanical pencil
- Backpack cover
- Large plastic trash bag

Backpack – Outside

- Sitting Pad wrapped around tent poles
- Water jugs-2
- Gloves
- Sandals
- Fleece jacket (under hood of backpack)

Wear

- Undergarments
- Liner socks
- Socks
- Hiking pants
- Belt
- Long sleeve T-shirt
- Hankie
- Ball Cap
- Hiking boots
- Gators
- Trekking poles (Carry)

Appendix Three
BACKPACK ILLUSTRATION

Backpack (From Front)

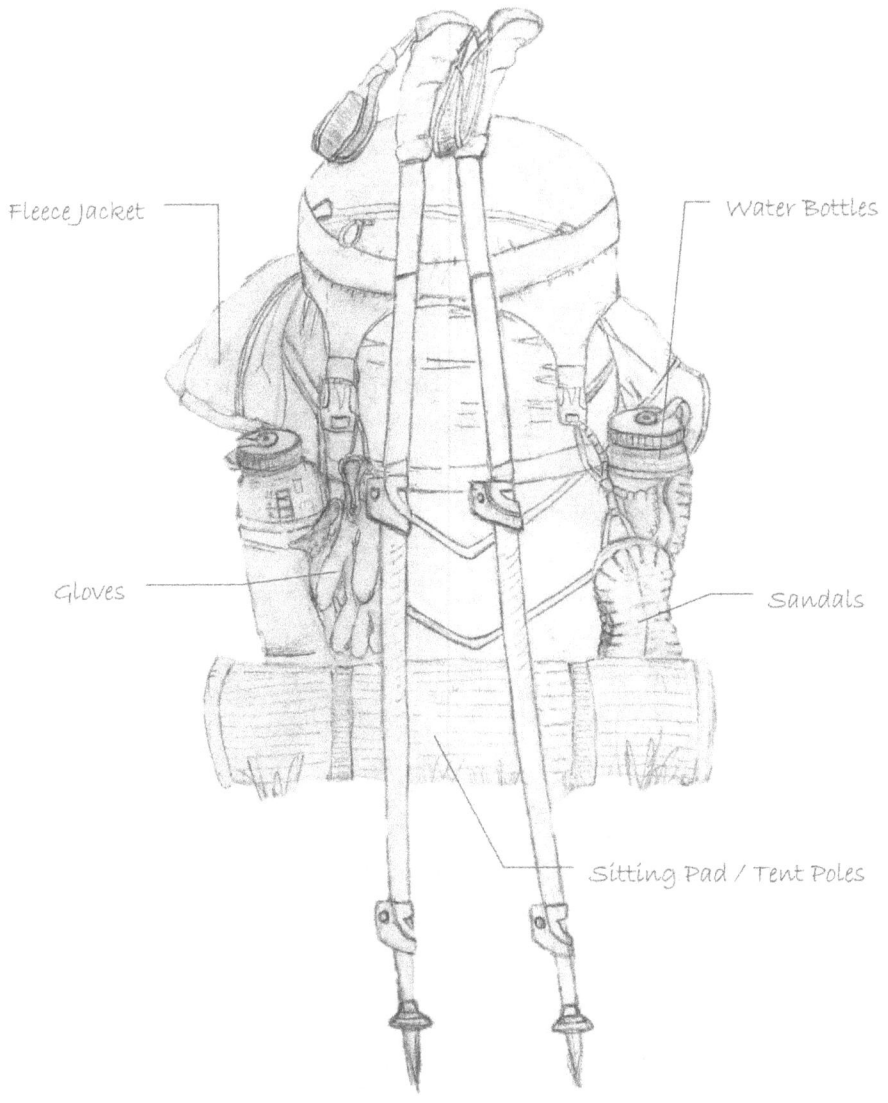

Backpacking & the Path of Life

Inside View of Backpack (From Side)

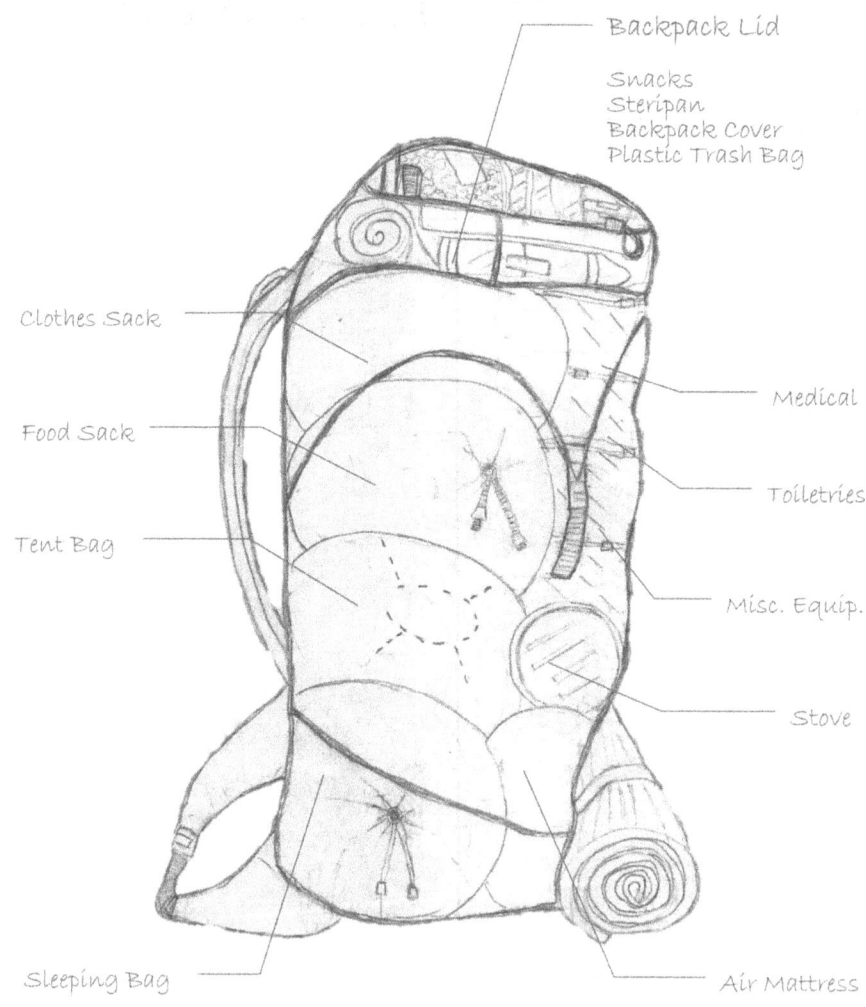

ABOUT THE AUTHOR

Dwayne Weaver is a man of deep faith whose love for the outdoors has defined his personal and spiritual journey. A devoted follower of Jesus Christ, Dwayne's life is rooted in his roles as a husband, father, grandfather, leader, and outdoorsman. For over 45 years, he has walked life's path alongside his wife, Cindy, raising their three daughters and now sharing in the joys of being grandparents to 10 grandchildren.

With a degree in Business and Accounting from Elizabethtown College, Dwayne built a successful career in the construction industry. His leadership roles, including Controller, VP of Finance, CFO, and CEO, are a testament to his professional competence and dedication. However, his passion for ministry was equally significant. After completing Bible courses through Global University, Dwayne became licensed for ministry with the Assemblies of God Church. He served as a Children's Pastor for seven years and held the position of Camp Program Director at a faith-based camp for underprivileged children, where he and Cindy helped introduce countless children to the beauty of God's creation.

Dwayne's passion for the outdoors is essential to who he is. Although he didn't begin backpacking until the age of 45, it quickly became a calling that profoundly connected him with nature and God. Whether fly fishing, hiking, or backpacking, Dwayne finds refuge and spiritual renewal in the wilderness. He cherishes these experiences not only as moments of adventure but also as opportunities for reflection and connection with his Creator.

Dwayne and Cindy reside in Pennsylvania, where they enjoy time spent with their family, church, and the great outdoors. For more information about Dwayne's adventures and downloadable resources, visit www.backpackingandthepathoflife.com.

www.ingramcontent.com/pod-product-compliance
Lightning Source LLC
Chambersburg PA
CBHW060526100426
42743CB00009B/1443